PRIMAL

Gourmet

RECIPES FOR PRIMAL LIVING

STEVE BENNETT & HANNAH ANDERSON

The Primal movement is gaining momentum, with more and more doctors recommending a Primal approach to living happily and healthily. *Primal Gourmet* is a simple guide to preparing healthy, nutritionally-rich foods, that will help you both look and feel great.

Bennett Health & Happiness Publishing (BHHP) is a not for profit organisation. All proceeds from the sale of this book will be donated to charities that further the cause.

ISBN: 978-1-9999071-4-3

Published December 2018
Book Design: Theo Johnson

www.bhhpublishing.com
www.primalcure.com

THE GREAT BRITISH HEALTH WARNING

As a nation, we are starving our bodies of good nutrition, and instead poisoning ourselves with mass-produced, artificially-modified, sugarloaded nonsense. In addition, we are using shampoos, antiperspirants and creams made with substances known to cause harm. Furthermore, we are stressed, don't sleep enough, yet are sedentary.

Our human body was not designed to live like this. As a result, British adults are now 2.5 stone (nearly 16kgs) heavier than they were just 50 years ago, and it won't be long before 1 in 2 is obese. Alarmingly, half our population at some point in their life will be diagnosed with cancer, and dementia has grown at an epidemic rate to become the biggest killer of women.

How have we ended up here? Well, much of what we currently believe to be healthy - or at least acceptable - has been shaped by misguided research, corporate greed and outdated governmental advice.

How do we avoid becoming a sick health statistic? We first accept that we have little evolved since our Primal ancestors and then realign both our diet and lifestyle to the fundamental needs of the human body. Welcome to the Primal way of living.

MORE SICK BRITAIN FACTS

Obesity will bankrupt the health service unless Britain gets serious about tackling the problem - **Simon Stevens, Chief Executive of the NHS**

We are the ONLY European country with a declining life expectancy - **Express.co.uk**

Obesity 'to be linked to more female cancers' than smoking - **BBC News**

The number of people diagnosed with diabetes in the UK has more than doubled in the last twenty years - **Diabetes.org.uk**

Almost four in five adults in England have a "heart age" older than their actual age - **The Guardian**

In the past year, 74% of people have felt so stressed they have been overwhelmed or unable to cope - **MentalHealth.org.uk**

A third of elderly patients may be being prescribed unnecessary medication, putting them at needless risk of side-effects and costing the NHS millions, a study has shown - **Telegraph.co.uk**

Studies show that up to one in 12 hospital admissions are medicines-related and two-thirds are preventable - **CareHomeProfessional.com**

Cardiovascular disease kills someone in the UK every 3 minutes - **hriuk.org**

"The Great British Health Warning is not written to cause stress. With a great National Health Service, our chances of living healthily and for a very long time are actually better now than ever before. However, to avoid becoming a sick statistic, it is crucial that you begin to live your life more in line with the needs of the human body. In practice, the more Primal you become, the happier and longer you should live.

All being well, you might even become a centenarian or even a supercentenarian."

Dr Shan Hussain and Dr Dan Maggs

ACKNOWLEDGEMENTS

When I started to live Primally a few years ago in order to get my health back on track, I needed inspiration in the kitchen, so I turned to the internet and bought lots of Paleo and Caveman diet books. To all of the chefs and authors who have inspired my cooking and thereby helped restore my health and dramatically reduce my waistline, I will always be deeply indebted. Over the past two years, my style of cooking has become very experimental and not always measured. I have continually tweaked and refined the dishes to the tastes and requirements of my family and therefore sadly I can't name all who have inspired me, as I don't recall the origins for many of my dishes.

To Hannah Anderson who joined the Primal team in 2017, a huge thank you for writing up many of the recipes and also for your fantastic food photography.

To my entire family, all 27 of you, for always being supportive, especially my wife who for the past few years has had to put up with my obsessive behaviour in researching what is Primal and what is not.

To my daughter Jessica, my wonderful niece Beth and my brother John, many thanks for your creative input in so many of my dishes.

To all of the wonderful doctors, authors, nutritionists and medical professionals, for giving up so much of their valuable time. To Theo for working on the great layout of this book, to Sian for all her editing skills and to Ashley for his lifestyle photos. Also, a massive thank you to James, the General Manager of *Primal Cure* and Dr Dan and Dr Shan for all of your hard work in helping me put the Primal books together. You are an amazing team and together we WILL make a difference.

CONTENTS

CONTENTS

CONTENTS

WHAT HEALTH EXPERTS ARE SAYING ABOUT LIVING PRIMALLY AND BOOKS BY THE AUTHOR OF PRIMAL GOURMET

DR MALCOLM KENDRICK | AUTHOR AND DOCTOR

"Fats are bad. Carbohydrates are good." – Based on this nonsense, dietary guidelines were created by those who didn't know the facts. The world of diet and health went mad seventy years ago; *The Primal Cure* is a refreshing ray of sanity.

Steve Bennett is bursting to tell the world about how he changed his diet and life around by looking at the lifestyle of our ancestors. I love his enthusiasm and I love the book. There is almost nothing here that I would disagree with – and that is remarkable for me. If you read *The Primal Cure* and take on board what is written, I can guarantee that you will be healthier, happier, slimmer and fitter.

DR EMER MACSWEENEY | RE:COGNITION HEALTH CEO & MEDICAL DIRECTOR

As more scientific studies highlight the important role that diet, exercise and lifestyle play in reducing the risk of developing Alzheimer's disease and other forms of psychological impairment, adopting *The Primal Cure* is a good way to protect both the brain and body in order to optimise your health. A simple solution to help maximise cognitive function and safeguard against diseases.

DR SHAN HUSSAIN | GP AND FOUNDER OF THE HEALTH STUDIO

The top five causes of death in the UK - namely cancer, heart disease, stroke, lung and liver disease - all have preventable elements to them. *The Primal Cure* brilliantly details how realigning our diet and lifestyle to that of our ancestors underwrites prevention.

DEBORAH COLSON | COGNITIVE NUTRITIONIST
The Primal Cure's approach to food, health, nutrition and exercise empowers individuals to take control of their own health. Steve Bennett's Primal principals reflect the way that we humans are designed to live, providing the basic foundations necessary for achieving a healthy mind and body.

DR DIMITRIOS PASCHOS | CONSULTANT PSYCHIATRIST
Modern pressures can seriously affect the mental health and psychological performance in people of all ages. *The Primal Cure* offers simple solutions to society's problems, by applying primitive principles to help us function at our maximum in today's world.

HANNAH RICHARDS | FOUNDER OF THE GUT CLINIC MAYFAIR, NUTRITION AND LIFESTYLE COACH
The Primal Cure contains a wealth of knowledge and busts some tired old fixed myths, exposing the truth about our diet and what it means to eat healthy, nutritious food. A great resource for anyone who wants to discover optimum health and improve their wellbeing.

DR JEFF STOKER | GP AND MASTER LIFE COACH
Never before has nutritional wellbeing and making the right lifestyle choices been so important. Historical doctrine, bad advice and poor dietary habits are crippling the health of today's society. *The Primal Cure* is one man's journey on a holistic approach to good health.

DR DAN MAGGS | GP AND FOUNDER OF CARB DODGING
The modern world is toxic. The influence of the big food and pharmaceutical corporations has corrupted our understanding of what it means to be healthy. Our nation is getting sicker. We all need to take charge and educate ourselves about our health. Steve Bennett is the perfect teacher. Read, learn, take action and your health will improve!

DR DAVID UNWIN FRCGP | NHS INNOVATOR OF THE YEAR
AMBASSADOR FOR THE ALL-PARTY PARLIAMENTARY GROUP ON DIABETES
SENIOR MEDICAL ADVISOR - DIABETES.CO.UK
FOUNDER MEMBER OF THE PUBLIC HEALTH COLLABORATION

I have been a GP in the north of England for 32 years, during which I have become fascinated by how people can become healthy without using medication. Imagine my surprise to find a book written by a non-medic which sets out so many of my beliefs so clearly!

At the heart of *The Primal Cure* is an interest in our basic needs both physiologically in terms of food and exercise, and psychologically in terms of our relationships with family and friends. As Steve Bennett explains, the logic behind so much of this is the 'hard wiring' left in us all by our ancient ancestors. Modern life is increasingly at odds with our fundamental design, resulting in so much of the chronic disease and unhappiness I see in clinical practice; where I have witnessed an eight-fold increase in type 2 diabetes, with terrible consequences for my community.

The good news? By following *The Primal Cure* and using the steps explained so well, I believe many illnesses can be avoided or possibly even reversed. Perhaps it is precisely because Steve is an intelligent layman and not a doctor that so many of the explanations in this book are so easy to understand. It is my hope that many of you will use this information to improve your own lives and the health of the people you care about around you.

Steve Bennett now
living Primally

ABOUT THE AUTHORS

Steve before going Primal

STEVE BENNETT

A family man and philanthropist, Steve admits to having spent most of his adult life overweight. But as a father of seven children, at the ripe age of 50 he decided to make a change. Author of *The Primal Cure* and founder of *Stone Aged Restaurant*, his *Primal Gourmet* food principles set the foundations for the restoration of his personal health and wellbeing; complimenting a healthy lifestyle and environment with good nutrition in line with that consumed by our ancestors.

HANNAH ANDERSON

As a respected fitness blogger and health enthusiast, Hannah's online reputation for living a healthy lifestyle centred around delicious plates of colourful food has gathered pace in just a few short years. A firm believer in the relationship between good nutrition and positive mindset, her success is fuelled by creative cooking principles which keep her fit, healthy and happy. Just 24 years old at the time of publishing, she's a wizard in the kitchen and her attention to detail is incredible. Most of all, Hannah believes in having fun with what we eat; cooking, the Primal way.

WHAT ARE PRIMAL FOODS?

As a species we evolve very slowly. **Have you ever wondered why it is that when we get out of the bath our fingers and toes are all wrinkly?** It's because thousands of years ago we used to catch fish with our bare hands and feet. To do so, our toes and fingers went wrinkly so that our feet could grip onto the rocks and fish did not slip through our fingers. **Do we need to do this today?** Perhaps not, but it's going to take our DNA a very long time to catch up.

The basis of living Primally is that we have to consume food in tune with the need of the human body. It is not about counting calories or eating what big food corporations marketing misguided and sometimes dishonest research tell us we should consume. It's simply about eating what nature designed for us to eat.

Primal food is inspired by organic nutrition consumed by various cultures according to the lifestyle of the human race before the agricultural revolution.

BRAINWASHED TO BELIEVE IN UNHEALTHY FOODS

How would you feel if I told you that most of what we have been conditioned and brought up to believe about food is simply wrong?

"We should eat a balanced diet." - **WRONG!** If you uncover something that's bad for your health you should avoid it. To get our weight under control and keep our health on track, we know for sure that we need to reduce our intake of both carbohydrates and processed foods.

"Never eat meat or fat as it causes heart conditions." - **WRONG!** Organic meat is one of the healthiest foods we can consume. In fact, it is what we are designed to eat.

"Eat three meals a day and eat little but often." - **WRONG!** Eating this way actually triggers disease as our body never goes into repair mode. Intermittent fasting is how we were designed to eat.

"Consume 0% or low-fat everything." - **WRONG!** We now understand that quality fats are not our enemy. Food labelled as low fat or zero fat are stuffed full of sugars to replace these missing fats, and it's these sugars that are deadly.

"Don't skip meals because your metabolism will slow down." - **WRONG!** Unless we go a whole four days without food, skipping meals actually speeds up our metabolism.

"Brown bread, brown rice and whole grain cereals are all healthy." - **WRONG!** They are actually unhealthy foods dressed up in a nutritional outfit. They still turn into sugar in our body and could eventually cause many to develop type 2 diabetes.

"Educate yourself on what food labels mean." - **WRONG!** Real food doesn't need a label.

"Prawns, eggs and other food high in cholesterol will raise your cholesterol levels and should be avoided." - **WRONG!** Just because a certain food type is high in dietary cholesterol, this has little correlation to what happens when you have consumed it.

"Artificial sweeteners don't make you put on weight." - **WRONG!** They might not in themselves be very calorific, but they damage our healthy gut bacteria and switch off the satiety hormone, which informs us when we are full. Therefore make us fat!

As a direct result of all of this brainwashing, as a nation we are very fat indeed. When Steve was born in 1966, only 11% of the British public were overweight and only 1.5% were obese. Today those numbers have risen to 64% and 28% respectively. The average UK adult weighs approximately 2.5 stone heavier than they were 50 years ago. As a direct result of all of this fatness and obesity, we are the only country in Europe with a declining life expectancy!

How do we get our health back on track? How do we start feeling happy with the way we look? We need to get a better understanding of what makes us healthy and what does not, and then tell the big corporates where to stick their harmful produce. We need to kick their carbohydrate and sugar-loaded foods into touch. Together we need to stop buying their hugely profitable packaged foods stuffed full of dangerous oils infused with chemicals and revert back to natural produce, like that consumed by our Primal ancestors; the type of which our bodies should be fuelled by design.

A NEW YOU

Every five or six years, you and I become almost an entirely new person. Our skin is constantly dying and being replaced - in fact our entire outer covering is replaced every single month. Our complete skeleton is regenerated every 10 years or so. Our lungs are replaced every six weeks, our liver in less than six months, and our tongue's 9,000 taste buds are rejuvenated every 10 days. Most of our body, cell-by-cell, day-by-day, is in a state of continual repair, rebuild or replace… or it should be.

All of this replacing, regenerating and rejuvenating is fuelled by one thing and one thing only: what we consume. Hence the saying, 'we are what we eat'. If we eat junk food, our new body parts will be created by junk and will not be as good or functional as the cells they are replacing. That's what causes ageing; rubbish input equals rubbish output. However, eat the right foods, drink enough water, get the right nutrients and we are going to make some pretty good body parts and at the same time delay the ageing process.

UNDERSTANDING MACRONUTRIENTS

To eat Primally, all it takes is a simple understanding of how the bulk of all food is created.

Why do we eat? There are two primary reasons. Firstly, in order to stay alive, from time to time we need to provide fuel to our organs. Secondly, to help repair and replace worn-out parts of our body, we need to consume certain minerals and vitamins. As it turns out, humans need roughly the same balance as all living animals. From koala bears to pigs, from giraffes to lions, from horses to humans, we all have similar needs when it comes to food and nutrition.

Nearly all ingredients of virtually everything we eat are made up of carbohydrates, fats and/or proteins. These three substances are known as macronutrients – derived from the Greek word 'macro', meaning large. Most natural whole foods are made up of just two of these macronutrients.

If the food (or drink) is derived from something that once had a face, it is made up of protein and fat, the exception being a small amount of carbohydrate in eggs and milk. If the food came out of the ground, it generally consists of protein and carbohydrates. Note how everything has protein! This is because protein is the building block of life.

A few exceptions to the two macronutrient rule are nuts, seeds, milk and avocados, which feature all three macronutrients. There are also a few foods made of just one macronutrient: table sugar (although it's less a food, more poison) is made up of just carbohydrate, and oils such as coconut and olive are made from just fat.

What do macronutrients do?

In all humans and animals, all three macronutrients can carry out energy-related roles:

1 - **Carbohydrates** are converted to sugar for energy
2 - **Fats** are converted to fatty acids, in the main to repair cells or to use as energy
3 - **Proteins** are converted to amino acids, to repair and rebuild cells or to use as energy

CARBOHYDRATES

All carbohydrates (which we call CARBS as an acronym for Carbohydrates Are Really Bad Sugars), whether they are simple or complex, unrefined or refined, eventually become sugar in the body. Without debating that some are worse than others, we need to understand that all CARBS – even those that are complex and unrefined – will at some point become sugar once digested.

Potatoes, pasta, bread and rice are all converted to sugar in the body. To our body, sugar is either used as an immediate source of energy or is stored as body fat! They might be dressed up in fancy packaging and often carry labels with misleading health benefits, but we need to realise our body was never designed to consume them, certainly not *en masse*.

Let's not beat about the bush. CARBS fulfil no purpose other than to provide energy or to store energy in the form of body fat. They don't help the body repair or rebuild cells and they possess zero nutritional value. Yes, ZERO! They don't contain any vitamins or minerals and they have zero benefits associated with them. In fact, quite the opposite, as all CARBS once in the body turn to sugar and too much sugar in the bloodstream can kill!

That's why we have the GI scale.

GLYCEMIC INDEX - If you are still not convinced that it's CARBS that make us fat with their constant and continual conversion into sugar, and their quick release into the bloodstream causing a spike in insulin, then why is there such a thing called the Glycemic Index? Food labels index all CARBS based on how quickly they perform this task. There is no glycemic index for either protein or fat. Why? Because protein rarely converts into sugar and fat never does.

First of all, the name 'glycemic' is derived from the medical term 'glycemia' meaning 'the presence of glucose in the blood'. All CARBS receive a glycemic index (GI) score from 1 to 100. The lower the number the better - or should I say, 'less horrible'. A score of 1 is the lowest and slowest and 100 is the highest and fastest to convert CARBS to glucose (sugar). Therefore, pure sugar obviously scores 100. However, it is not as black and white as the GI score might suggest, as it assumes we are only eating the food being scored in isolation and not combining it with other foods, which when bound together after digested may change the speed of conversion into sugar.

The other limiting factor of GI is that it doesn't look at portion sizes. There are some items with a fairly low GI score, where the portions sizes are by definition big and therefore still not recommended if we are either trying to lose weight or stay healthy. A more reflective index is the glycemic load (GL). While GI is useful to know how quickly glucose will enter the bloodstream, the GL informs us how dangerous that load will be.

CARBOHYDRATES - THE GL INDEX

The charts compare the GI and GL of most foods we find in the UK. We have tried to use portion sizes that are fairly conservative. So for example with white bread we have used just one slice, but if we were to eat two, then simply double the GL figure.

Food	GI	Serving size	GL per serving
Lucozade, original (sparkling glucose drink)	95	250ml	40
Baked potato	85	1 medium (173g)	28
White rice, boiled	64	1 cup (186g)	33
Macaroni and cheese	64	1 serving (166g)	30
Raisins	64	1 small box (43g)	20
Spaghetti, white, boiled 20 mins	42	1 cup (140g)	16
Bagel, white, frozen	72	1 small bagel 70g	25
Rice Krispies	82	1.25 cups (33g)	23
Fanta, orange soft drink	68	250ml	23
Spaghetti, white, boiled, average	46	1 cup (180g)	22
Sweet potato	54	1 cup (133g)	12
Pizza	30	2 slices (260g)	13
Instant oatmeal, average	79	1 serving (250g)	21
Boiled white potato, average	82	150g	21
Coco Pops, average	77	1 serving (30g)	20
Corn Flakes, average	81	1 serving (30g)	20
Dates, dried, average	42	Handful (60g)	18
Snickers bar, average	51	60g	18
Sponge cake, plain	46	1 serving (63g)	17
Rice cakes, average	82	1 piece (25g)	17
Spaghetti, whole-grain, boiled	42	1 cup (180g)	17
Instant mashed potato, average	87	1 serving (150g)	17
Coca Cola, (US formula)	63	250ml	16
Brown rice, steamed	50	1 serving (150g)	16
Sweet corn on the cob	48	1 piece (60g)	14
Oatmeal, average	55	1 serving (250g)	13
Quinoa, cooked	53	1 cup (150g)	13
Cheerios	74	1 cup (30g)	13
Corn tortilla	52	1 serving (50g)	12
Apple juice, unsweetened	41	1 cup (248g)	12
Orange juice, unsweetened	50	1 cup (248g)	14

The GL index is calculated simply by multiplying the typical grams of carbohydrates in a serving by the GI index for that type of CARB and then dividing it by 100.

Food	GI	Serving size	GL per serving
Potato crisps, average	56	1 bag (40g)	12
Hot chocolate	51	1 cup (28g)	12
White bread (white flour)	75	1 slice	11
Banana, raw, average	52	1 large	14
Bran Flakes	74	3/4 cup (29g)	13
Corn chips, plain, salted	42	1 serving (50g)	11
Pitta bread, white	68	1 piece (30g)	10
Muesli, average	56	1 serving (30g)	10
Kidney beans, average	34	1 cup (150g)	9
Ice cream, regular, average	62	1 cup (72g)	10
Microwave popcorn, plain, average	65	1 serving (20g)	7
Chicken nuggets, frozen, reheated	46	4 pieces (100g)	7
Baked beans	40	1 serving (150g)	6
M&M's, peanut	33	1 handful (30g)	6
Apple, average	38	1 medium size	6
Oranges, raw, average	45	1 medium size	5
Tomato juice, no sugar added	38	1 cup (243g)	3
Milk, full fat, average	31	250ml	4
Watermelon	72	1 serving (120g)	4
Green peas	54	1 cup (80g)	4
Strawberries	40	1 cup (152g)	4
Grapefruit	25	1/2 slice	3
Chickpeas	10	1 cup (150g)	3
Cashews, salted	22	2 handfuls (50g)	3
Carrots, average	39	1 piece (80g)	2
Beansprouts	25	1 cup (104g)	1
Soy beans, average	15	1 cup (150g)	1
Peanuts	13	2 handfuls (50g)	1
Broccoli, cabbage, celery, cauliflower, green beans, mushrooms, spinach, almonds, hazelnuts, macadamia, pecan, walnuts, beef, chicken, eggs, fish, lamb, pork, veal, shellfish, lobster, turkey, ham	0	As much as we like	0

All brand name data was taken from www.health.harvard.edu on 12th April 2017

PROTEIN

Protein comes from the Greek word 'prota',
meaning 'of primary importance'. All proteins
get converted into amino acids inside the
body. There are 22 different types of amino
acids, all created from the elements carbon,
hydrogen, nitrogen or sulphur.

Our body can make all but nine of these amino acids, and these nine
are extremely important for our health. That's why they're called the
'essential proteins', and we must make sure they form part of our
regular diet. Without consuming these, the ability of our body to repair
itself and rebuild cells and organs will be compromised.

FATS

Most of our recipes include fat. But doesn't fat cause cholesterol and heart disease? Actually not! Fat has been demonised for far too long. It is not the villain. For more info, go to the PrimalCure.com website or visit our channel on YouTube to watch our interview with Dr Malcolm Kendrick, author of *The Great Cholesterol Con*.

Fat does not make us fat! The villain who broke in and messed up most people's slender body was Mr CARBS.

Just like there are those nine essential amino acids that we need to consume in order to survive, it is also essential that we consume both saturated and unsaturated fats/oils.

However, while some fats are healthy for us, others are outright dangerous. How did fat get such a bad rap? Well, 50 years ago when mass-manufactured deadly trans fats and

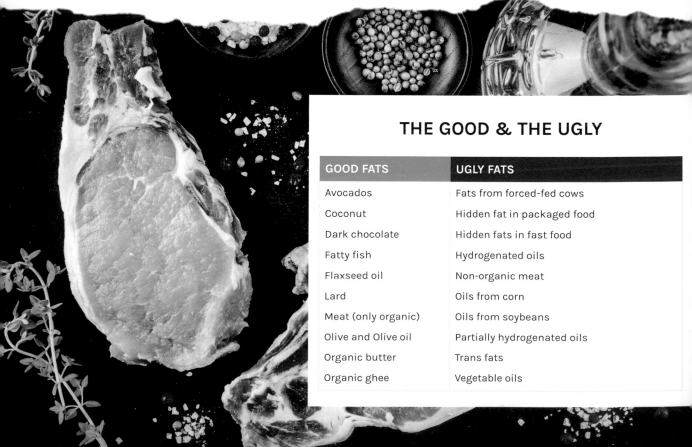

THE GOOD & THE UGLY

GOOD FATS	UGLY FATS
Avocados	Fats from forced-fed cows
Coconut	Hidden fat in packaged food
Dark chocolate	Hidden fats in fast food
Fatty fish	Hydrogenated oils
Flaxseed oil	Non-organic meat
Lard	Oils from corn
Meat (only organic)	Oils from soybeans
Olive and Olive oil	Partially hydrogenated oils
Organic butter	Trans fats
Organic ghee	Vegetable oils

hydrogenated oils started to appear *en masse*, some misguided and ill-informed individuals lumped all fats under the same heading, and deemed them all unhealthy. Yet, natural animal fats vs factory-created, chemically-enhanced fats is like comparing chalk and cheese.

In the incredibly insightful book *Smart Fats*, written by Dr Steven Masley and Jonny Bowden PhD, CNS, they write, "We've been so concerned with 'saturated fats vs. unsaturated' and 'animal vs. vegetable', that we've lost sight of a far more important distinction: toxic vs. non-toxic fat – or, as we call it, dumb fat vs. smart fat".

Not only are most fats healthy for us, they are so much better at making us feel full. Unlike CARBS, which spike our glucose and insulin levels, and then bring them crashing down shortly afterwards making us crave even more food, fat leaves us feeling full for longer – much longer. The reason for this is that it isn't processed in the stomach, but instead has to wait until it reaches the intestines. Fat, just like a balloon, floats on water. The enzymes that break down fat are lipases. Lipases struggle to get at the fat in the stomach while it's floating on top of the watery mush being tumbled in our internal washing machine, and patiently wait for it to drop into the intestines. While the body is busy processing carbohydrates and protein, the sidelined fats make us feel fuller for longer.

The only difference between oils and fats is that oils are liquid at room temperature.

FAT/OIL	SMOKE POINT	GOOD FOR
Avocado oil	271°C	Use for frying, searing and roasting or as a tasty salad dressing
Coconut oil (refined)	232°C	Great for everything! Contains 66% MCTs
Flaxseed oil	107°C	With its low smoking point, it's best not to be used for cooking. An excellent source of Omega 3 (4:1 Omega 3 to Omega 6 ratio) and tastes great over salads or add to a smoothie
Ghee	252°C	62% saturated fat, has a distinctive flavour, excellent for frying
Hazelnut oil	221°C	A great all-round oil for cooking and applying to the skin
Hemp seed oil	165°C	Add a smooth, nutty taste to salad dressings and marinades
Lard	188°C	Lard is most definitely a Primal fat. Makes the best fried chicken
Macadamia oil	210°C	A great all-rounder for both cooking and applying to the skin
Olive oil (extra light)	242°C	Use for frying, searing and roasting or as a tasty salad dressing
Olive oil (extra virgin)	191°C	Use for frying over medium heat. Or as a salad dressing
Olive oil (virgin)	199°C	Use for frying over medium-high heat. Or as a salad dressing
Organic butter	120-150°C	Use to add flavour in low temperature cooking
Seasame seed oil	210°C	A great all-round oil for cooking and applying to the skin

FIBRE

How important is fibre to our health? According to The American Journal of Clinical Nutrition – consuming 35g of fibre was associated with a lower risk of cardiovascular disease by as much as 54% and death from all causes by 37%.

What is fibre? It's the rough guys who hang around with macronutrients. In fact it's so rough that our bodies can't break it down and therefore fibre makes us feel full without extracting any energy (calories). Fibre is also used as a vehicle to transport micronutrients around our body. In addition, fibre is absolutely crucial to colonise our microbiome with friendly bacteria. You can learn more about the importance of the microbiome in our book *The Primal Cure*.

Here is a quote from the website of our amazing National Health Service, "Fibre is an important part of a healthy diet. It can help prevent heart disease, diabetes, weight gain and some cancers, and can also improve digestive health".

However, as we don't eat cereals, bread, oats when living Primally, we need to ensure we get plenty of fibre from shirataki, nuts, seeds, vegetables, fibre supplements and certain fruits.

ORGANIC

Meat - When it comes to animal produce, it is critically important to buy as natural as we can possibly afford. I am sure you have heard the saying 'we are what we eat' but, when it comes to animal produce, the saying should be extended to 'we are what our food eats'. Free range eggs, free range chicken and grass fed cows all provide us with heaps of benefits. They are rich in vital vitamins, and have a really healthy Omega 3 to Omega 6 balance. Cows, pigs, chickens and lambs that are allowed to live naturally, in their natural habitat, feeding on their native Primal diet, are really good for our health.

Fruit and vegetables - Why is it recommended that we eat our five daily fruit and veg? One of the main reasons is that they contain something called antioxidants and these are very important in helping prevent many diseases. Especially cancer. Any fruit or vegetable that manages to survive its harsh environment is full of powerful antioxidants. Those that aren't wither and die and are therefore never consumed. But when a fruit or vegetable is protected by pesticides, their natural antioxidants aren't necessary and don't develop. Various experts have written articles on the differing quantity of antioxidants found in fruits that are organic compared to semi-manufactured varieties, and I put the median average of all of their reports at about 9:1. In other words, on average an organic fruit is nine times more beneficial than an enhanced fruit.

DAIRY PRODUCE

Part of the secret to avoiding many diseases lies in the maintenance of our healthy gut bacteria.

Some 2,500 years ago Hippocrates, the father of modern medicine, taught, 'All diseases begin in the gut'. I believe Hippocrates was in fact way ahead of his time, and that many diseases really do begin in the gut. There is something in our modern society that is causing mass murder of certain bacteria in our stomach.

Whether it is diet, pollution, pesticides, starch, microwaves, fast food, fizzy drinks, ready meals, overly prescribed medicines, hydrogenated oils, incessant snacking, sugar or any one of the multitudes of modern world problems, something is upsetting the balance of our ecosystem at an alarming rate.

This is where dairy enters the scene and where Primal living takes a divergence from those following a strict Paleo diet. In order to defend and indeed rebuild the body's ecosystem – the microbiome – it's beneficial to eat a diet rich in fibre and fermented foods. While fibre is taken care of with choices such as nuts, seeds and lots of leafy greens, in the modern diet fermented foods are generally absent without leave! Three of the top five fermented foods are derived from dairy – probiotic live yoghurts, fermented milk known as kefir and certain cheeses.

GUIDELINES FOR VITAMINS AND MINERALS

In addition to consuming macronutrients, it's also necessary to top up our biological system with certain nutrients that are going to make it run smoothly, efficiently and for as long as possible. These are known as micronutrient and are primarily divided into two groups; vitamins and minerals. The more nutritionally dense our food, the more healthy we will ultimately look and feel.

Alongside all vitamins and minerals mentioned below you will see the official daily recommended amount that we should consume. But let me warn you that all of these values are founded on the basis of deficiency. Set by a panel of EU nutritional experts, the recommended Nutritional Reference Values (NRVs) are said to represent the required intake levels of all vitamins and a selection of minerals to help prevent deficiencies in the vast majority of healthy people in Europe. We should consider the NRVs like we do a minimum wage, it's kind of a safety net, an entry point, not necessarily the amount anyone would really desire.

VITAMINS	NRV
Vitamin A (retinol)	800 mg
Vitamin B1 (thiamin)	1.1 mg
Vitamin B2 (riboflavin)	1.4 mg
Vitamin B3 (niacin)	16 mg
Vitamin B5 (pantothenate)	6 mg
Vitamin B6 (pyridoxine)	1.4 mg
Vitamin B7 (biotin)	50 µg
Vitamin B9 (folic acid/folate)	200 µg
Vitamin B12 (cobalamin)	2.5 µg
Vitamin C (ascorbate)	80 mg
Vitamin D (cholecalciferol)	5 µg
Vitamin E (tocopherol)	12 mg
Vitamin K	75 µg

µg - Microgram   mg - Milligram

MINERALS	NRV
Calcium	800 mg
Chloride	800 mg
Chromium	40 µg
Copper	1 mg
Fluoride	3.5 mg
Iodine	150 µg
Iron	14 mg
Magnesium	375 mg
Manganese	2 mg
Molybdenum	50 µg
Phosphorus	700 mg
Potassium	2000 mg
Selenium	55 µg
Zinc	10 mg

PRIMAL SUPERFOODS

On the next few pages we will detail all of the foods that we consider to be perfectly Primal and can be consumed without the need to count calories.

ALMONDS

An excellent source of phytonutrients, fibre, copper (necessary for producing red blood cells), magnesium, calcium, zinc and selenium. Makes a fantastic flour for baking and a healthy alternative to milk.

ANCHOVIES

They are full of mineral goodness including calcium, selenium, iron and magnesium, plus they're loaded with Omega 3, riboflavin, niacin, folate, vitamin E, vitamin B6, vitamin B12, vitamin A and vitamin K.

APPLE CIDER VINEGAR

Full of friendly bacteria and acetic acid, apple cider vinegar aids weight loss, reduces LDL cholesterol and helps to lower blood sugar levels. Some studies suggest that vinegar can kill cancer cells and shrink tumours.

ASPARAGUS

It is believed to be the finest natural aphrodisiac. It contains aspartic acid, known to neutralise the excess ammonia in our body which is often a root cause of a drop in libido.

AUBERGINE

Also known as eggplant, they are actually a fruit and not a vegetable. They are a rich source of anthocyanins, a pigment with antioxidant properties that can protect against cellular damage and free radicals.

AVOCADO

It is a unique fruit in that it is primarily a fat. There are so many benefits of regularly consuming avocado, that if we had to take just one fruit on a desert island, it would win hands down.

BAKING SODA

Made from pure sodium bicarbonate. Helps maintain a healthy pH balance throughout the digestive system. Helps with digestion and promotes healthy bowel functions. Also helps to reduce acid reflux.

BEEF (ORGANIC)

Rich in Omega 3 and possibly the very best source of protein. Grass fed beef also contains a secret healing component called conjugated linoleic acid (CLA), which amongst other benefits assists in burning body fat.

BELL PEPPER

Also known as capsicum. A yellow one contains roughly the same amount of vitamin C as five whole oranges! A red bell pepper equates to three oranges and the green bell pepper, contains twice that of an orange.

BLACKBERRIES

Just like strawberries, they are very sweet but don't contain many calories. Their nutritional value is tremendously high, with one cupful containing 30% of our fibre, and 50% of our vitamin C daily needs.

BLUEBERRIES

Possibly the most highly antioxidant substance you can swallow is the highly praised and delicious blueberry. They are rich in the flavonoid anthocyanin, which is responsible for their vivid colours.

BOK CHOY

Ranks as one of the highest sources of nutrients per calorie of all vegetables. It's stuffed full of antioxidants which studies have shown to lower the risk of developing lung, prostate, breast and colon cancer.

BONE BROTH

It contains an amino acid called glycine, which plays an important role in the health of our skin, our digestive system, circulatory and nervous system, muscle growth and repair and in managing our hormones.

BRAZIL NUTS

Offer an abundant source of selenium, which is a powerful antioxidant that protects the immune system.

BROCCOLI

Without doubt, broccoli is the ultimate vegetable and one that everyone needs to learn to love, especially raw. One portion has more vitamin C than an orange and more calcium than a glass of milk.

BRUSSELS SPROUTS

Sprouts increase the production of proteolytic enzymes. These make the digestion of both carbohydrates and proteins a lot easier. Sprouts are also known for boosting our metabolism, alkalising the body and helping to prevent both cancer and heart disease.

BUTTER

Has been demonised over recent decades but is in fact super-healthy as long as it originates from organic grass fed cows. Great for frying with as it has a high smoking point.

BUTTERNUT SQUASH

Technically a fruit and not a vegetable, butternut squash contains a huge amount of vitamin A which is good for the maintenance of the immune system and good vision, plus vitamin C, E, B6, thiamine and much more.

CABBAGE

Due to its high content of phytonutrients, cabbage has been shown to cure stomach ulcers. These compounds strengthen stomach muscles, which helps fight back against acid attacks. Rich in vitamins C and K.

CARROTS

They really do help us see in the dark! They are rich in beta-carotene that the liver converts into vitamin A, which when it reaches the retina, is converted to rhodopsin, a pigment that helps enhance night vision.

CASHEWS

Packed full of fibre, protein, antioxidants, minerals and vitamins. They are a rich source of vitamins including thiamin, riboflavin, pantothenic acid, pyridoxine, riboflavin, vitamin E and vitamin K.

CAULIFLOWER

Its wealth of phytonutrients and anti-inflammatory compounds fight off heart disease, ward off cancer and help us to lose weight. It is also rich in carotenoids, which help maintain healthy eyesight.

CAYENNE PEPPER

A type of chilli pepper that is closely related to jalapenos. It both helps to boost metabolism and reduces hunger. Making it great to add to dishes of you are trying to lose weight. Also believed to lower blood pressure.

CELERY

Used for centuries as a medicine, celery contains an array of phytonutrients that help lower blood pressure and prevent heart disease and inflammation. They're full of electrolytes that help prevent dehydration.

CHEESE

Those made from raw milk and haven't been pasteurised are a brilliant source of naturally fermented goodness. Soft cheeses are especially rich in helpful bacteria and can cure many smaller digestive issues.

CHIA SEED

One of the most popular superfoods in the world, chia seeds are extremely rich in fibre, Omega 3, protein and minerals. Gram for gram chia seeds contain more Omega 3 than salmon!

CHOCOLATE

Where the cacao content is higher than 70%, it increases insulin sensitivity, protects against type 2 diabetes, lower blood pressure, support brain functions such as memory and much more.

COD

From the same family as haddock and pollock, cod provides a rich source of iodine, selenium, phosphorus, vitamin B12, B3, B6 and a great source of protein. The fish is also rich in healthy omega 3 fatty acids.

COFFEE

A recent study suggests that regular coffee drinkers are less likely to fall victim to Alzheimer's disease. Its high concentration of polyphenols make it a great antioxidant too.

COURGETTE

Known as Zucchini in the USA, it is rich in vitamin C, vitamin B6, riboflavin, folate, magnesium and much more. It contains many antioxidants and anti-inflammatory phytonutrients.

CRANBERRIES

Full of vitamin C, manganese, vitamin E, vitamin K1 and copper. Contains a potent dosage of quercetin, which supports brain health, is anti-inflammatory and studies have linked it to the prevention of certain cancers.

CUCUMBER

Contains antioxidants that support our immune system and are excellent for balancing hormone levels. Its phytonutrients are said to reduce the risk of cardiovascular disease as well as several types of cancer.

EGGS

Contain everything needed to create life! They include all nine essential amino acids, vitamins A, B12, B2 and B5 as well as lots of minerals. They are full of good fats and many other traces of helpful nutrients.

FLAXSEED / LINSEED

Seen as the king of the plant world for its high levels of Omega 3. It also contains lots of fibre and protein as well as many other vital nutrients. Can be ground to make flaxseed flour (also known as flaxmeal).

GARLIC

Famed for its ability to lower blood pressure. There is also research that suggests its antioxidant power is one of the best at helping to prevent cancer. For acne sufferers, it cleanses the skin from the inside out.

GHEE

To make ghee, water is evaporated (clarified) out of butter, leaving behind a higher concentration of fat and making it more suitable for cooking at higher temperature.

GINGER

This miracle root is brilliant for curing sickness and digestive problems. Ginger is also known to reduce pain far more effectively than many pain killers. Very efficient at reducing discomfort during the menstrual cycle.

GOJI BERRIES

Regarded by many, as the most healthy fruit on the planet. Said to protect our eyes and immune system. Studies have shown that they protect against certain cancers and improves depression, anxiety and sleep.

GRAPEFRUIT

Its bitter taste is full of antioxidants and fibre, making it one of the healthiest citrus fruits we can eat. Several reports are emerging that suggest that it might help in preventing cells from becoming insulin resistant.

GREEN PEAS

Also known as garden peas, they are full of disease-fighting antioxidants, fibre and protein. Also a very good source of vitamin K, manganese, vitamin B1, copper, vitamin C, phosphorus and folate.

HADDOCK

A saltwater fish that is an extremely rich source of protein and packed full of essential vitamins and minerals. A great source of Omega 3, vitamin B6 and B12, magnesium, niacin, phosphorus, and selenium.

HAZELNUTS

Exceptionally rich in folate (vitamin B9), which is a unique feature for this essentially British nut. Helps to reduce the bad LDL cholesterol and increase the good HDL. If cold pressed properly, makes a great cooking oil.

HEMP SEED

Hemp seeds are known for having one of the most balanced nutritional profiles among all the seeds. They are an excellent source of Omega 3 and if cold pressed, makes for a great edible oil.

HOT PEPPERS

Also known as capsaicin, it is also used to treat various skin conditions. Today, its miracle cure is so widely acknowledged that we can purchase it as a supplement or a topical cream that we apply to our skin.

KALE

Stuffed full of sulphur, calcium and iron, kale is great for detoxifying our body and promoting a healthy liver. It protects our cardiovascular system, lowers our blood pressure and acts as a natural antidepressant.

LAMB

An excellent source of protein and Omega 3 fatty acids. It's rich in minerals such as zinc, iron, selenium, phosphorus, potassium, copper and magnesium, plus it's a great source of vitamin B12, B3, B6 and B5.

LEMON & LIMES

Their concentration of antioxidants helps prevent free radicals and therefore reduces the likelihood of many cancers. A phytonutrient called limonin, literally halts inflammation and many common illnesses.

LENTILS

Whilst they do contain carbohydrates, they offer vegetarians a good source of fibre, folate, iron, manganese, potassium, zinc, phosphorus, magnesium, copper, vitamin B1 (thiamin) and vitamin B5.

LETTUCE

Romaine has 10 times more vitamin A than Iceberg. So to look after our skin or teeth, we should choose Romaine over Iceberg. It is also more concentrated in vitamin K, therefore helps to protects against cancer.

LUCUMA

A yellow-fleshed South American fruit which packs a powerful health punch with its amazing abundance of fibre, antioxidants, vitamins and minerals.

MACADAMIA NUTS

Provide a perfect Omega 3 to Omega 6 balance. They contain palmitoleic acid, which improves fat metabolism and therefore assists weight loss. They reduce the likelihood of heart disease and stroke.

MACKEREL

A typical 80g piece provides us with the following amount of our NRV. Vitamin D 201%, sodium 148%, vitamin B12 160%, vitamin B6 15%, magnesium 12%, potassium 11%, iron 6% and calcium 5%.

MANGO

Packed full of 20 different vitamins and minerals including, Helps to lower blood sugar levels and boost cognitive health. Its combination of magnesium, potassium and sodium, helps to naturally lower blood pressure.

MUSHROOMS

Rich in protein and fibre and an excellent source of vitamins D, B, C, calcium, selenium and potassium. They support our immune system and, amongst other things, are said to help prevent certain cancers.

OLIVES

Olives and their oil are a staple part of the Mediterranean diet, where their lifestyle and food choices dramatically reduces the occurrence of heart attacks, and leads to a disproportionate number of centenarians.

ONIONS

They are also full of phytonutrients which protect against many unhealthy strands of bacteria. They are thought to help prevent certain cancers and lower the risk of diabetes and neurodegenerative disorders.

PEANUTS

They have an amazing antioxidant we don't find in other nuts - resveratrol. It's an antioxidant believed to help prevent both heart disease and certain cancers. Don't eat too many though, as they are very calorific.

PECAN NUTS

An excellent source of protein, fibre and heart-healthy antioxidants. The nut supports bone development and can help protect the cardiovascular system.

PINEAPPLE

Rich in vitamin C and an excellent source of manganese. The richest source of bromelain, a mixture of enzymes that are anti-inflammatory and which studies suggest protects against tumours and cancer.

PISTACHIO NUTS

High in protein and fibre and a good source of phosphorus, copper and potassium. As they are rich in a specific amino acid called L-arginine, they can help improve blood flow in clogged arteries.

POMEGRANATES

Rich in vitamin C, vitamin K and potassium, studies have shown that they may help reduce the risk of cancer and all kinds of inflammation. They are also said to help treat high blood pressure and hyperglycemia.

POPPY SEED

The iron and phosphorus contained within the poppy seed is essential for muscle and bone maintenance. Regular consumption helps boost immunity, lowers bad cholesterol, fights anxiety and depression.

PORK

An excellent source of vitamins such as vitamin B3, B1, B2 and B6, plus minerals phosphorus, selenium, zinc, iron, potassium and magnesium. Pork offers a great source of protein without any carbohydrates.

POULTRY

All poultry, chicken, turkey, duck etc, are great sources of protein. They also provide lots of nutrients such as iodine, iron, zinc, vitamins (especially B12) and essential fatty acids.

PUMPKIN

A rich source of potassium which has a positive effect on blood pressure. Its antioxidants beta-carotene help to prevent degenerative damage to the eyes and may reduce the risk of developing certain types of cancer.

PUMPKIN SEED

Pumpkin seeds are rich in protein and B vitamins such as thiamin, riboflavin, niacin, pantothenic acid, B6 and folate. They also contain vitamins E, K and C as well as Omega 3 fatty acids.

RASPBERRIES

They are full to their capacity with cancer-fighting antioxidants. They are said to more concentrated in antioxidants than tomatoes and boost our mood and help us retain our memory as we age.

SALMON

Have you noticed how some fish becomes dry even if we just slightly overcook it, yet salmon always appears to remain moist? That's the huge amount of Omega 3 holding the fish nicely together in our frying pan.

SARDINES

Also known as Pilchards, they help defend against depression, fight against cancers, improve our moods and memory, protect our heart, stave off Alzheimer's and Parkinson's disease and so much more.

SEAWEED

Full of calcium, folate, iodine, magnesium and a whole host of vitamin Bs. Recent research suggests that seaweed, which is also full of fibre, is great for our guts and helps slow down digestion.

SESAME SEED

Help in preventing diseases like arthritis, asthma, migraines, osteoporosis and certain cancers. Due to their high content of essential fatty acids, they are also extremely beneficial to the health of our skin. Great as a cooking oil.

SHELLFISH

Prawns, oysters, mussels, clams and shrimps have numerous benefits for our health, in particular they are a rich source of selenium and vitamin B12.

SHIRATAKI NOODLES

Comes from the konjac plant and is largely composed of glucomannan, which is a water-soluble fibre. It holds water so well, that when cooked it looks like pasta or noodles, but contains virtually zero calories.

SPINACH

A terrific source of antioxidants, full of minerals such as iron, potassium, zinc, as well as vitamin A, E, K and vitamin B9 (folate). Nitrate in its leaves is the secret behind its muscle-building properties.

SPRING ONIONS

Due to its highly beneficial sulphur content green onions have been used for centuries in Chinese traditional medicine. They provide a rich source of vitamin C, B2, thiamine vitamin A and vitamin K.

SQUID

Full of protein and healthy fats. Rich in niacin and vitamin B12 is important for red blood cell production and the health of the nervous system. Not so beneficial when bought as fried calamari!

STRAWBERRIES

Very British, and very good for our health. Full of flavour and fibre, it often surprises many people how truly healthy strawberries are. For some reason, many believe they are full of sugar. They aren't!

SUNFLOWER SEED

With vitamin E and copper found in abundance, as well as many other vitamins and minerals being very much present, sunflower seeds are extremely good for our health and longevity.

SWISS CHARD

Contains 12 different powerful polyphenols which can reduce the damage caused by free radicals, and slow down the ageing process. Contain syringic acid, which is known to regulate blood sugar levels.

TEA

Green tea especially is full of epigallocatechin gallate (ECGC), which speeds up our metabolism while at the same time suppresses hunger. It increases adrenaline, which in return produces heat and therefore burns calories.

TOMATOES

Believed to contain thousands of different phytonutrients, which suspended in their vividly coloured skin support a healthy heart, boost our immune system and may even reduce the risk of cancer.

TROUT

Evidence suggests that eating fish such as trout is associated with a lower risk of stroke and is possibly beneficial for mental health, for example to improve mood and help treat depression.

TUNA

Whether it is in a can or a fresh slice of raw tuna, this fish is full to the brim with goodness. When in a can we shouldn't buy it with added oil, as when we drain it we also drain away a lot of the Omega 3.

TURNIPS

Great for preventing colds and flu, as well as promoting healthy hair and skin. A rich source of zeaxanthin and lutein. Lutein has been nicknamed 'vitamin eye', as it promotes and protects healthy eyesight.

WALNUTS

As they are full of Omega 3, walnuts are good for the heart. They are also rich in L-arginine, they can help improve blood flow in clogged arteries. If cold pressed properly, makes a great cooking oil.

WATERCRESS

Used more than 2,000 years ago by Hippocrates to treat patients in hospital, it is an incredibly powerful natural medicine. It has more calcium than milk, more iron than spinach and more vitamin C than oranges!

WHEY PROTEIN

A great source of essential amino acids and other healthy nutrients. The benefit of consuming whey goes way beyond just building muscles and increasing strength. Studies show that it helps in reducing body fat.

YOGURT

Without doubt, a totally natural fermented yoghurt is full of millions of nature's tiny miracles, and adding just a small daily portion to our diet can do wonderful things for our gut flora.

PrimalCure™
LIFE BEYOND THE CAVE®

To help you achieve the very most out of your nutritious cooking, *Primal Cure* offer a unique range of fine quality primal products and ingredients.

When you place your order, no matter how small, even if it's just for a single jar of coconut oil or flaxseed oil, we will send you a free copy of Steve's book *The Primal Cure* (*worth £9.99*), just use the code <u>GOURMET</u> at checkout.

WWW.PRIMALCURE.COM

BRITAIN IS SICK

1 IN 2 PEOPLE TO BE DIAGNOSED WITH **CANCER**
25% SUFFER WITH **MENTAL ILLNESS**
HEART DISEASE IS THE BIGGEST KILLER
DIABETES RATES HAVE DOUBLED IN 20 YEARS
AND IS **OBESITY** *ABOUT TO BANKRUPT THE NHS?*

THE
PRIMAL CURE
AVOID BEING A SICK

STEVE BENNETT SECOND EDITION

COCONUTS

We have given coconuts their own page as they top the Primal superfood list.

Before we get going, I want to touch on a few things first. Recently, coconuts have been receiving a little negative press, with some misguided researchers suggesting their fat content leads to high cholesterol and heart disease. Ridiculously, these reports are just recycling old news where they linked saturated fats to heart diseases, which as we have already read has never been established (especially for totally organic saturated fats).

Coconuts are highly beneficial for our health as they contain vitamins B1, B3, B5, B6, C and E, and come jam-packed with healthy minerals such as calcium, selenium, sodium, magnesium and phosphorous. What's more, they're full of fibre, which today is sadly lacking in most diets in most British diets.

Coconut Oil - There are several thermogenic supplements you can take that turn you into a fat burning machine, but one of the most effective fat burning triggers is simply coconut oil. Coconut is a saturated fat and also an MCT (Medium Chain Triglyceride). MCTs are the fats that just keep on giving! When consumed they turn almost immediately into fuel, help the body convert body fat into energy and help suppress hunger. I personally put a tablespoon in my morning black coffee for a great kick start to the day. If you can find coconut oil that is cold pressed at a very low temperature, just like *Primal Cure's* very own coconut oil, then you will love their wonderful flavours.

Coconut Flour - If it wasn't for the holy coconut, making bread without grain flour would be kind of difficult. Derived from the dried flesh of the coconut, this is a flour packed with fibre, protein and healthy fats. It's free of both gluten and grain, and it can be used to make tasty breads or cakes, pancakes and desserts. You can also use it to thicken up sauces and curries, and add it to smoothies to ensure you are getting your daily fix of healthy fat.

Coconut Cream & Milk - Unlike cow's milk, coconut milk is completely lactose free! Not to be confused with coconut water, coconut milk and cream is produced by grating the coconut flesh and then soaking it in hot water. The thick cream rises to the top, where it is skimmed off, and the remaining juice can be filtered and bottled as milk. Why is it so beneficial? Well, it's no normal fat. It's the richest source of medium-chain fatty acids (MCFAs), which is the closest thing for sale in a can or bottle to human breast milk!

Coconut Water - This is the actual juice extracted from the shell of a young coconut before it develops into flesh. Coconut water contains less than 3g of natural fructose per 100g. Compared to Coke at 11g, it sounds virtually sugar free! And there is less sugar in a glass of coconut water than in an orange!

Coconut Chunks Or Flakes - Both are great to snack on, put into salads or add awesome flavour to curries. I will often sprinkle flakes in with nuts or a bowl of berries topped with probiotic yogurt.

Desiccated Coconut - The definition of desiccated means to remove moisture from something that normally contains moisture. Desiccated coconut is produced from drying the shredded coconut and then heating it. It's unsweetened and as none of the fat is removed, all of its amazing health benefits are preserved.

Coconut Aminos - Soy sauce is a popular ingredient especially in Chinese and Japanese cuisine. However, its not primal and for those looking to avoid gluten, Coconut Aminos makes for a wonderful alternative. It's a dark coloured sauce made from coconut sap and as the name suggests, it's rich in amino acids, as well as vitamin C and several vitamin B's.

HERBS AND SPICES

Herbs and spices have been used for centuries as medicines in cultures from Asia to the Native Americans, from Southern Europe to the Aztecs. While for thousands of years, herbal practitioners had no idea why or how herbs actually worked, they became extremely successful at identifying the right herb for the right aliment through trial and error.

What I love about using them in my cooking is that they add flavour to just about anything. And flavour is really important. I recommend you experiment with as many herbs and spices as you can get your hands on. Even better still, get out in the garden and grow your own. There is no more a satisfying meal than one where we know the flavour was created in our own backyard.

Plus, when we are trying to encourage our family and friends into a Primal way of living, tantalising their taste buds with herbs and spices makes it easy in helping them convert to our healthier lifestyle.

WHEN WE ARE NOT
FEELING WELL, WE
SHOULD FIRST LOOK FOR
THE CURE IN OUR SPICE
RACK AND NOT IN OUR
MEDICINE CABINET.

PRIMAL CURE

BASIL
The antioxidants in basil make it a natural anti-inflammatory, and are believed to help the body fight off cancer.

BAY LEAVES
According to IJNC, bay leaves are believed to help fight against colorectal cancer.

BLACK PEPPER
Improves digestion and promotes intestinal health. Used for centuries for their anti-inflammatory and anti-flatulent properties.

CINNAMON
Cinnamon provides a rich source of minerals including calcium, copper, iron, manganese and zinc. It contains vitamin A, vitamin C and vitamins B1, B2 and B3.

CORIANDER
Coriander is said to be good for our cardiovascular system and can aid in lowering blood pressure.

CUMIN SEEDS
Used in traditional medicine. Promotes weight loss and improving blood sugar levels and cholesterol.

LEMONGRASS
A rich source of antioxidants, that have anti-inflammatory properties, that are associated with reduced risk of cancer.

MACA ROOT
There are numerous benefits to maca roots, including increasing libido and reducing erectile dysfunction.

MUSTARD SEEDS
It helps our digestive system function properly. And its strong taste helps relieve the symptoms of colds and flu.

NUTMEG
Said to relieve tension and anxiety, making it an excellent aphrodisiac. Also said to help detoxify the body.

OREGANO
The list of medical benefits of oregano is so extensive that there are now many oregano oil supplements.

PAPRIKA
A spice created from grounding up different varieties of Capsicum peppers.

PARSLEY
Helps the thyroid function normally and is said to reduce the spread of cancer by preventing tumours from growing.

ROSEMARY
Said to boost memory retention and other cognitive functions, and thought to help delay the onset of dementia.

THYME
Lowers blood pressure and can improve moods. It has been used for centuries to treat bronchitis and the common cold.

TURMERIC
Turmeric is one of the most powerful natural medicines we can add to our food. Period!

VANILLA
Rich source of antioxidants including vanilla acid and vanillin, providing the herb with anti-inflammation properties.

WHITE PEPPER
Rich in antioxidants, reduces inflammation and promotes proper digestion. Also decreases blood pressure.

WHAT TO EAT
...IN MODERATION

Legumes One of the areas that *Primal Cure* differs from the Paleo way of living is in our views on legumes. Firstly, there is growing evidence to suggest that our Primal ancestors consumed certain beans and other legumes, such as peanuts (yes, surprisingly peanuts are legumes and not nuts), as part of their diverse diet.

If we abstained from legumes, we couldn't have dark chocolate and who would want to miss out on dark chocolate? And a chilli con carne would not be a chilli con carne without kidney beans. Plus, I would personally find it too difficult to live life without the occasional handful of peanuts.

While most legumes do contain CARBS, they are rich in protein and fibre and are often very advantageous to the bacteria in our microbiome. Many are full of vitamins and minerals, making them highly nutritious. One of the reasons legumes sometimes receive a bad press is because they often contain phytic acid/phytate, which binds minerals together in our digestive system resulting in lower quantities being available for the body to absorb. However, some experts suggest that phytate itself may contain protective properties against cancer, diabetes and cardiovascular disease. With the jury still out, my advice is to consume legumes in sensible quantities.

Salt Just like fat, salt has had a bad rap over the past few decades, but it is in fact essential to our health. As we begin to follow the principles of *Primal Cure*, we will be eating fewer processed foods and therefore we might need to check whether we are actually consuming enough salt. It is certainly unlikely on a *Primal Cure* lifestyle that we will be taking in too much.

Fruit Berries made it onto our Superfood list because they are simply awesome, so too did the amazing avocado (which is technically a berry as well). Most other fruits are also healthy, but because of their high sugar content just be sure to eat them in moderation.

Rhubarb It is a vegetable and not a fruit. Full of vitamin C and vitamin K, along with potassium and manganese. In China it is commonly used as a medicinal herb. It is quite high in CARBS, so don't eat too often.

Sultanas and raisins High in fibre, rich in nutrients and full of beneficial antioxidants. However, they are also high in sugar. So must not be eaten in excess and should be avoided if you are trying to lose a lot of weight.

Coconut Sugar Also known as coconut palm sugar, is not made from the coconut itself, but from the sap of the tree. Like regular sugar, it is high in carbohydrates, but unlike sugar they aren't empty calories. They contain zinc, calcium, potassium and a rich source of antioxidants. That said it's high in fructose (It has a GI of 35), so use sparingly.

Honey Unlike sugar, which contains zero health benefits (what is known as empty calories), honey provides a rich source of antioxidants, which amongst other health benefits help to lower blood pressure. But as it does contain sugar, just don't consume too much of it.

WHAT NOT TO EAT

CARBOHYDRATES

*Throughout this book you will see carbohydrates written as CARBS. The reason for this is that I want you to see carbohydrates for what they are, with a very apt acronym: **'Carbohydrates Are Really Bad Sugars'**. What do I mean by this? Basically, carbohydrates are just sugar in disguise. Potatoes, pasta, bread and rice all convert to sugar in the body and, to the body, sugar is poison! They might be dressed up in fancy packaging, and often carry labels with misleading health benefits, but we need to realise our body was never designed to consume them.*

Avoid carbs As many vegetables actually contain carbohydrates, and we'll never be able to avoid them completely. But this just makes it all the more important to avoid all CARBS that are derived from foods lacking good nutrition. All CARBS that have been cultivated since the agricultural revolution, aka potatoes, pasta, bread and rice are all too quickly converted to sugar in the body and must be avoided if you want to enjoy a slender healthy body.

CARBS Digestion 101: All CARBS are converted to sugar, and any excess sugar in the blood is bundled up with insulin and stored as BODY FAT. This can happen so quickly that shortly after a CARB-loaded meal, we feel hungry again. We call this the Carbocoaster.

The Carbocoaster works like this. We eat a McDonald's burger and the body converts the bread roll to sugar. Our brain summons insulin to quickly grab any excess sugar, which to our body is pure poison, and stores it as fat. Because the bread roll is now no longer in circulation, we feel hungry again, so consume another. The Carbocoaster effect is enhanced because both the blood sugar levels keep getting topped up and then depleted quickly, and after the initial surge of insulin this too plummets as it finishes hiding the sugar. This rollercoaster only happens with CARBS and other sugars. There is no Fatocoaster or Proteinocoaster, just the dangerous, highly addictive, adrenalin-rushing, body-crushing, high-speed Carbocoaster. As a nation, we need to get off this ride as quickly as we can as it is making us hungry, sick and very obese!

WHAT NOT TO EAT

GRAINS

Avoid grains Just like CARBS, grains get easily converted into sugar in our digestive tract. But aren't they full of healthy fibre? Yes they are, however, just like the strawberries in strawberry ice cream might be good for us, there are other ways of getting our strawberries without eating bucket-loads of sugary ice cream. We should get our fibre from nutritionally-rich sources such as nuts, seeds and greens, but not from grains. Grains, just like CARBS, spike our insulin levels and turn to fat on our waistline faster than you could possibly imagine.

Hang on a minute, what about whole grain and brown rice – aren't these proven to be good for us? Sorry, no. They might be marginally less bad for us than their heavily processed brothers, but they still aren't Primal and therefore our body is not designed to eat them. At the end of the day, while they might have a little more nutritional value, it's still just mutton dressing up as lamb.

One more thing. I hate to be the bearer of bad news, but corn isn't a vegetable – it's another form of grain. While corn on the cob might not be as unhealthy, as most of it normally passes straight through the body - popping perfect little yellow cubes out in our poo - just like other grains and CARBS, those pieces that do become digested are converted into poisonous sugar. In fact, stop and think about this for a moment. Since the mid 1960s, scientists in America have been able to genetically modify corn so much, that it is now used across the globe as a sugar (high-fructose corn syrup) in packaged foods. Corn syrup will most likely one day in the future be regarded as an even bigger killer than cigarettes.

WHAT NOT TO EAT

SUGAR

Avoid deadly sugar

It is thought that Primal man developed a bit of a sweet tooth by occasionally finding fruit, and in some regions, honey. When he did, he gorged on them. Remember, he didn't have a way of refrigerating food, so he just sat there and scoffed down as much as he could. It is therefore our early ancestor's fault, if you like, that we are programmed through our DNA to enjoy gorging on sweet things. But before you start thinking that it is therefore Primal to eat loads and loads of sugar, remember that for our ancestral caveman, the fruit would only be available once a year!

When we eat sugar, we are not consuming anything helpful. Sugar does not possess any of the vitamins or minerals our body requires. Zero! Just like cigarettes and booze, sugar is addictive. Just like cigarette manufacturers stuff their cancer-causing products full of addictive nasties, food manufacturers put sugar into almost everything these days. From baked beans to canned meats, from sauces to even bottles of supposedly healthy water. Make no bones about it - food manufacturers attempt to get us addicted to their products by adding sugars.

While these food manufacturers are really clever and have all sorts of marketing spins, with a little knowledge we can spot the deadly white stuff even if it has been well hidden. On food packages, pretty much every word that ends in '-ose' is a sugar. Maybe it's a subliminal acronym for something like 'other sugar exposed', or buyer beware 'obesity sugar exists'. Dextrose, fructose, galactose, glucose, lactose, maltose and sucrose are all simply different types of sugar. As well as watching out for the deadly '-ose', treat all syrups with the same contempt. They are all high in sugar, with heaps of calories that offer minimal nutritional value.

PRIMAL ANALOGY: It is said that if a frog is put into a jar of boiling water, it will jump out immediately, but if the frog is put into cold water which is then brought to a boil slowly, it will not perceive any danger and will be cooked to death. It's the same with sugar. It doesn't kill you immediately, but both poisons and ages you, just a little bit every time you eat it.

Artificial Sweeteners

Have you seen how tiny these things are? One tiny little pill, less than quarter the size of a Tic Tac, makes our coffee or tea taste like we have put several spoons of sugar in it. The fact that these artificial pills are so tiny yet so powerful immediately suggests that something can't be right with these lab-engineered alternatives. Caveman never ate anything manufactured in a laboratory, so do you really think we are designed to eat anything artificial?

It is also believed that artificial sweeteners cause untold damage to our microbiome, causing good bacteria to run for the hills and leaving the bad guys to flourish. Plus, while the liver is dealing with inbound artificial sweeteners, it has to temporarily suspend producing the satiety hormone leptin.

WHAT NOT TO EAT

PROCESSED FOODS AND GMO'S

Processed food Caveman didn't have anything processed at all. Everything was fresh, almost fresh or rancid. I went to a supermarket with four of my children and asked them to spend an hour thinking about what percentage of food in the shop was processed. Together, we arrived at the conclusion than nine out of ten items of food in a supermarket are indeed processed.

But is that a problem? Of course it is, because we are not designed to eat processed food. Packaged food can last weeks, months, sometimes years before it needs to be consumed. How is that possible? They stuff it full of nasty preservatives. Generally speaking, the longer the shelf life, the more preservatives are in the food. While these preservatives might provide extended shelf life, they tend to kill the helpful bacteria in our gut. Think about it, how do you extend the shelf life of food? You add chemicals that kill off bacteria. However, there is no safety mechanism in these foods to make sure they exclusively kill off bad bacteria. Woefully, once they enter our gut they kill millions of healthy bacteria that, over thousands of years, nature has ensured we keep alive in our body to fight off both diseases and infections.

Genetically Modified Organisms How un-Primal are genetically modified organisms (GMO)? Did our ancestors sit in caves with a chemistry set gluing together different bits of plants in an attempt to produce strawberries in December? Of course not, they were simply too busy hunting and gathering! How common are GMO foods? Regrettably very! Nearly all websites quote corn, soy and sugar to be the most widely consumed genetically modified foods. The statistics are staggering. In the USA 95% of sugar, 94% of soybeans and 88% of corn is from modified crops.

SUMMARY OF UNHEALTHY NON-PRIMAL FOOD

Here is a list of what food to avoid if you want to look and feel healthy.

Artificial Sweeteners	Fizzy Drinks	Rice
Barley	Flour	Rye
Bread	Grains	Soy
Cakes	Milk Chocolate	Spaghetti
Cookies	Oats	Sweets
Biscuits	Packaged Food	Sweetened Beverages
Cereals	Pasta	Sugar
Corn	Plastic Bottled Water	Trans Fats
Corn Syrup	Potatoes	Vegetable Oils
Fast Foods	Processed Foods	Wheat

- PRIMAL -

Breakfast

BERRY NICE PRIMAL OATMEAL

 Number of servings: 4   Preparation Time: 5 minutes   Chilling Time: 1 - 2 hours or overnight

Although we're not big breakfast fans, we know that this isn't the case for everyone living a Primal lifestyle. Some of you will find that your body works perfectly well without breakfast; some of you will find that you don't. If you're one of those who rely on breakfast in the mornings, then our Berry Nice Primal Oatmeal is for you.

What if we told you that you could still enjoy a bowl of creamy oatmeal in the morning whilst still staying true to a Primal lifestyle? You'd think we've gone bonkers but believe us, with this recipe it really is doable. This one's grain free and contains a healthy dose of protein and good fats, making it the perfect natural breakfast fuel. Unlike many supermarket breakfast options, this recipe is free from refined sugar, carbohydrates and contains no funny ingredients.

If we're honest - leaving all Primal thoughts aside - we much prefer this version of the classic oatmeal recipe. Thanks to the chia seeds and coconut flour, you really don't miss out on the creaminess of the original recipe and in fact, the texture is far better than your bog standard recipe. You've got crunch, you've got nuttiness and you've got a lovely sweetness from the raw honey. Nothing wakes you up in the morning quite like this breakfast.

Ingredients

OATMEAL
280ml almond milk
6 tbsp chia seeds
125g mixed nuts
1 tbsp coconut flour
2 tbsp mixed seeds (pumpkin seeds,
flaxseeds and hemp seeds)
2 tbsp raw honey

TOPPINGS
2 tbsp full fat natural yoghurt
Handful of fresh berries
1 tsp raw honey

Method

Begin by pulsing your nuts until finely chopped.

In a mason jar, add your chia seeds, your pulsed mixed nuts, coconut flour and mixed seeds. Pour the almond milk into the jar, along with the honey and stir until everything has combined. You may also wish to shake the jar. Pop in the fridge for an hour or two to allow the oatmeal to set.

Once done, remove from the fridge. You should have a thick oatmeal texture. If not, leave for a little longer in the fridge (overnight can often be best). If the texture is a little thick, then simply add a dash of almond milk and mix.

Serve your oatmeal with a dollop of full-fat yoghurt (the natural kind), a handful of berries and an extra dash of raw honey if you please. Enjoy!

Primal on nuts

It shouldn't come as a surprise when we tell you that nuts are in our list of Primal superfoods. All nuts are rich in protein and healthy oils such as Omega 3. Most of them also contain beneficial levels of magnesium, potassium, iron, copper and various B vitamins. When it comes to nuts, the most natural, unprocessed nuts are the ones we should be looking for. Ditch the salted, processed and roasted ones.

3-IN-1 BREAKFAST EGG MUFFINS

 Number of servings: 6   Preparation Time: 10 minutes   Cooking Time: 20 minutes

You can find tonnes of breakfast egg muffin recipes online but I'd like to think that the ingredients we've chosen are not only Primal-friendly, but provide us with essential vitamins, minerals and antioxidants. Whether you're a breakfast fan or just need a little extra boost throughout the day, these breakfast egg muffins are a mouth-watering saviour and are packed with all the breakfast flavours you could possibly ask for. Plus, there are three to choose from!

Our favourite muffin has got to be the sundried tomatoes with maca and watercress. The watercress pairs beautifully with the sundried tomatoes, adding a peppery taste to the egg muffins. The maca powder on the other hand, complements the flavours further with a slight nuttiness. Some can identify the taste of maca whilst others, can't. Really, we've only added the ingredient for the extra nutritional boost rather than the taste.

Ingredients

EGG MIX
10 eggs
Black pepper and salt to taste

BACON, CHEESE, MIXED SEEDS AND CHILLI MUFFINS
20g gruyere cheese
3 bacon medallions
1 tbsp mixed seeds
1/4 tsp fresh chilli (finely diced)

SUNDRIED TOMATO, MACA AND WATERCRESS MUFFINS
65g chopped sundried tomatoes
1 tsp maca powder
10g watercress

GARLIC MUSHROOMS AND SPINACH MUFFINS
35g mushrooms
20g spinach
1 tsp chopped garlic
Sprinkle of black pepper

Method

Begin by pre-heating your oven to gas mark 4 (180 degrees Celsius) and if following the bacon and cheese recipe, grill your bacon medallions under the grill until crispy.

Whilst your bacon cooks, crack the eggs and whisk them until you have a foamy mixture. Pour the mixture into your well greased 12 hole muffin tray and be sure to fill each muffin hole halfway. Combine the bacon and cheese filling mixture and divide this equally into four, and add to four of the muffin mixture. Repeat this process for the sundried tomato and maca, and garlic mushroom and spinach fillings. You should end up with four bacon and cheese muffins, four sundried tomato and maca muffins and four garlic mushroom and spinach muffins.

Once done, pop your breakfast egg muffins in the middle of the oven to bake for 20 minutes. Once your muffins are cooked and no longer jiggle in the middle, remove them from the oven to cool. To keep these fresh, pop them in an airtight container in the fridge and consumer within 3-5 days. Enjoy!

Primal on maca

Many people don't know this but maca is in fact a vegetable and has been used in tribal medicines for thousands of years. Maca is native to the Andes Mountains in Peru and is related to the likes of broccoli, cauliflower and kale. It's normally consumed as a ground powder and is particularly delicious in smoothies and Primal-friendly hot chocolates! Personally, we think the taste of maca varies depending on the ingredients it's paired with in a recipe. For example, pair maca with a healthy dose of cacao powder and you can create a truly delicious caramel flavour. However, pair it with something a little more savoury, sundried tomatoes for example, and you'll experience its nutty flavour.

GARLIC MUSHROOMS AND SMOKED SALMON TOPPED WAFFLES

Number of servings: 2   **Preparation Time: 5 minutes**   **Cooking Time: 10 minutes**

If you're a waffle lover and thought that transitioning to a Primal lifestyle meant that you had to give up your beloved pancakes with carbs, then think again. Thanks to our garlic mushrooms and smoked salmon topped waffles recipe, you can enjoy waffles the Primal way.

To make the waffles themselves, you'll need only three ingredients: cream cheese, eggs and a little coconut flour. They're light, filling, full of delicate flavours that complement the salmon and garlic mushrooms and overall, this dish is packed with healthy fats and protein. All you need are the chosen ingredients listed below, a blender and a decent waffle maker. Don't worry, it's not as time consuming as it sounds. You'll simply blend the waffle ingredients together, fry the garlic mushrooms whilst the waffles cook, and bam. In 10 minutes you'll have yourself a delicious and healthy Primal breakfast.

Ingredients

90g cream cheese (natural)

2 large eggs

1 tsp coconut flour

2 tsp dill (optional)

4 slices smoked salmon

4 large mushrooms (sliced)

1 tbsp extra virgin olive oil

2 cloves garlic (finely chopped)

4 pinches pepper

2 cups spinach

Method

Begin by mixing the cream cheese, eggs, coconut flour and 2 pinches of pepper together in a blender.

Once blended, pour the waffle mixture onto your hot waffle iron and close. Cook until your waffle maker instructs you to lift the griddle. Repeat this process until you've used up all your mixture.

Whilst your waffles are cooking, heat a pan with extra virgin olive oil and add the slices mushrooms with garlic. Cook until golden and soft. Add the spinach and wilt.

Serve your waffles up between two and evenly split the spinach, mushrooms and salmon (2 slices each) onto each plate. Add the dill on top of the salmon and sprinkle with the rest of your pepper across both plates. Dig in!

Primal on cheese

One of the few areas where Primal takes a different path from Paleo, is our love of cheese. Many people believe that cheese is full of lactose and sugar, however, when cheese is fermented the lactose (sugar) is significantly reduced. Furthermore, the longer the cheese is aged, then the more it provides you with a healthy bacteria which ferments even more lactose. So yes, you can indeed enjoy some waffles in moderation as part of a Primal lifestyle.

PROTEIN ACAI CHIA PARFAIT

🍴 Number of servings: 1   🕐 Preparation Time: 5 minutes

In this recipe, we've used the powder of a recently popular superfood berry – acai. They look like a mix between a grape and a blueberry. The seed itself takes up about 80% of the berry and the flesh and skin contain tonnes of vitamins and nutrients.

Ideally, when it comes to this pudding it's best to prepare the night before for a thicker texture. Don't worry though, you'll only need 2 minutes to prep the chia pudding and it's done. Come morning time you'll be left with a deliciously sweet chia pudding that's ready to be layered into a healthy and nutritious parfait that will take no longer than 2 minutes.

You have two options for the yoghurt part. To make it a high protein breakfast, simply add a scoop of organic WHEY protein powder and mix it together. Or, if you're not fussed by adding extra protein (the yoghurt and chia seeds will already contain protein), then simply top your chia pudding with the yoghurt mixed with acai powder and sprinkle on some seeds and berries. Our favourite go-to fruit.

Ingredients

CHAI PUDDING
1/4 cup chia seeds
1 cup milk of choice
1 tsp raw honey

PROTEIN YOGHURT
170g full fat natural yoghurt
1/4 tsp acai powder
1 scoop WHEY protein powder - unflavoured
1 handful mixed berries
1 tbsp mixed seeds

Method

Begin by preparing the chia pudding overnight.

Place all ingredients into a bowl, mix and leave in the fridge to set overnight or for a few hours.

In the morning, pour the chia pudding into a jar.

For the protein yoghurt, simply mix together the WHEY, yoghurt and acai powder until combined.

Layer on top of the chia pudding (or have full-fat yoghurt on its own) and top your parfait with mixed seeds and a handful of berries. Enjoy!

Primal on breakfast

When living a Primal lifestyle you have two options when it comes to breakfast. You can either skip it (especially if you're intermittent fasting) or you can start the day with a Primal-friendly breakfast that's high in fats and protein and will leave you feeling full and ready to tackle the day ahead.

NUT N' CLUSTERS PRIMAL GRANOLA

🍴 Number of servings: 6   🕐 Preparation Time: 5 minutes   🕐 Cooking Time: 10 minutes

Granola is one of the UK's most-loved cereal options. But, surprisingly, it is also one of the unhealthiest. So do not be fooled, Primal friends! Whilst granola may appear healthy with clever labelling, stating 'oats', nuts and fibre', it's actually packed full of sugar, saturated fats and CARBS. So no, despite popular opinion, it's not the healthiest option first thing in the morning!

For our nut n' clusters Primal granola recipe we've simply swapped out the oats for almond flour, replaced sugar with raw honey, and combined everything with our favourite, healthy brain-boosting nuts - pecans, walnuts and pecans. The combination of the nuts, raw honey and almond flour are what allow the clusters to form. In fact, without the almond flour, the clusters wouldn't exist so please do not miss this essential ingredient!

Be careful though, this recipe is addictive, that's the only way to describe it. It's sweet, it's nutty, it tastes just like the real thing and most importantly, it's crunchy! The best thing about our granola is that it's incredibly versatile, and you can add whatever you like to it (as long as it's Primal-friendly).

Ingredients

65g almonds
60g brazil nuts
60g pecans
80g flaked almonds
55g almond flour
1 pinch salt

1 tsp cinnamon
1/2 tsp ginger
1/4 cup raw honey
1 vanilla pod
1 tsp coconut sugar (optional)

Method

Begin by preheating your oven to gas mark 3 (160 degrees Celcuis).

In a bowl, add all of your ingredients together and mix (slowly) until clusters start to form together. Be sure not to over mix as this will break up the clusters.

Once your clusters have formed, line a baking tray with parchment paper and lay out your granola.

Pop in the middle of the oven to bake for 15 minutes (or until golden and crunchy), remove from the oven and leave to cool.

Serve with some milk (or milk of choice) or enjoy as a simple nutty snack! This granola is best kept in an airtight container for up to a week.

Not a fan of almond?

Then simply swap it for coconut flour. However, you may find that you'll need a little extra honey! Either way, we hope you enjoy this recipe as much as we enjoyed making it Primal-friendly!

Kids love it if you...

If you're slowly introducing your children to a Primal lifestyle, as well as driving them away from the sugary cereal boxes, then add a few shavings of 80%+ dark chocolate to the recipe. Not a lot, but a little to make it even more enticing and delicious.

SMOKED SALMON EGG BAKE

🍴 Number of servings: 1   🕐 Preparation Time: 2 minutes   🕐 Cooking Time: 15 minutes

This smoked salmon egg bake is quite possibly the easiest breakfast recipe you could prepare for yourself in the morning. It's a popular recipe in the Paleo world, therefore it's a heavily inspired recipe. Have no doubts though, just because it's easy, it's still a delicious breakfast recipe and thanks to its high Omega-3 intake, it's a dish that will leave you feeling full and satisfied all morning long.

This recipe is high in fats, high in protein and very low in carbs, making it the ultimate Primal dish to start the day with. It's also very adaptable so feel free to mix up your seasoning. We've used dill as it's delicious paired with fish and if you're yet to try it, we seriously urge that you do!

Ingredients

1 - 2 slices smoked salmon
2 large eggs
1 cup spinach
1/3 cup of full fat milk

Salt and pepper to taste
2 pinches worth dill
1 wedge lemon

Method

Begin by preheating your oven to gas mark 4 (180 degrees Celsius).

In a bowl mix together your spinach and milk.

In an oven-proof dish, add your salmon and spinach and then crack two eggs on top.

Season your dish with pepper and salt and then top with dill.

Place in the middle of the oven to bake for 15-20 minutes (longer if you like your eggs hard).

Once done, remove from the oven, serve with a lemon wedge and dig in!

Primal on smoked salmon

Some will argue that smoked salmon is a processed meat and therefore not truly Primal. We say that as long as it's not from a farm, then there's no reason to be concerned by the smoking process. Smoked salmon is still a great source of protein, healthy fats, B vitamins, vitamin D, magnesium and selenium. And most importantly of all, due to its high concentration of omega-3 fatty acids, salmon has also been known to lower the risk of heart disease and alzheimer's disease.

COCONUT AND MACA PRIMAL PANCAKES

🍴 Number of servings: 1   🕐 Preparation Time: 2 minutes   🕐 Cooking Time: 15 - 20 minutes

These coconut and maca primal pancakes have increasingly become a new favourite recipe in the Bennett household. Despite being grain free, they're still incredibly fluffy and light. In fact, they're just like your usual American pancakes - minus the unhealthy fat, grease, and CARBS!

To make these Primal-friendly pancakes we've used a gift from the heavens (or a very tall tree), coconut flour. If it weren't for the holy coconut, making bread without grain flour would be kind of difficult. Derived from the dried flesh of the coconut, this is a flour that's packed full of fibre, protein and healthy fats. It's free of both gluten and grain, which makes it easy for us to avoid CARBS.

Ingredients

2 tbsp coconut flour
2 tbsp almond flour
1 tbsp maca powder
1 tsp coconut sugar
Pinch of salt
2 large eggs

5 tbsp milk
1 tsp coconut oil for cooking
1 tbsp full fat yoghurt
Handful of blueberries
1 tbsp mixed seeds

Method

Begin by whisking your eggs in a mixing bowl until extremely fluffy and bubbly (this is important for the fluffiness of the pancakes).

Next, add the flours, maca powder, coconut sugar and salt and mix everything together.

Add the milk one tablespoon at a time, stirring in between each tablespoon. Dependant on the coconut flour you're using, you may need more or less milk. Therefore, it's important that you make sure to stir in between.

Once you have a pancake mixture, do a final whisk and leave for 5 minutes to set.

During that time you can heat a pan with a tsp of coconut oil until the pan becomes hot.

On medium heat, add a tbsp of pancake mixture to the pan and create a pancake shape. Once bubbles appear, flip the pancake and cook for a further 2-3 minutes. Repeat this process until all of your pancake mixture has been used up.

Serve your pancakes with a handful of blueberries, seeds and a tbsp of full fat yoghurt - if you wish

BANANA AND ALMOND PROTEIN PANCAKES

🍴 Number of servings: 1   🕐 Preparation Time: 5 minutes   🕐 Cooking Time: 10 minutes

---

American style pancakes. They're fluffy, they're creamy and they're extremely mouthwatering, but they're also full of sugar and CARBS, right? Wrong! Well, in this instance anyway. These creamy banana and almond protein pancakes are not only low in CARBS, but they're also high in protein – making them the perfect post-workout breakfast meal.

What will surprise you the most is that they taste just like the real thing. They're creamy (thanks to the organic grass fed whey), they're extremely fluffy and they have just the right amount of sweetness too, thanks to the natural sugar of the banana. On top of that, they're low carb, full of healthy fats (thanks to the almond flour) and they contain only 5 main ingredients – almond flour, WHEY, 1 banana and 2 eggs. That's it!

So if that's not an easy morning breakfast idea that's fun for all the family, then we don't know what is! We topped our pancakes with a few extra banana coins, fresh blueberries and a little almond butter (great for the kids). It's healthy, but it sure doesn't taste like it!

Ingredients

1 medium banana sliced
20 grams whey protein powder
30 grams almond flour
1 tbsp almond flour
1 vanilla pod (optional)

2 medium eggs
1/4 medium banana sliced and for topping
1/3 cup blueberries for topping
1 tsp almond butter

Method

In a bowl whisk together your eggs until foamy. Add the sliced banana and mix the egg and banana together until you have almost no banana lumps.

Add the almond flour and whey protein powder and whisk everything together once again. If you're using a vanilla pod then add this too.

Heat a frying pan with a tsp of coconut oil and make sure that the entire pan is well greased with a tissue. Using a tbsp, add a dollop of pancake mixture to the pan and cook on medium heat until bubbles start to appear and then quickly flip. Cook for another minute or two on the other side and then repeat this process until you've used up all your pancake mixture.

We keep our pancakes in the oven on a warm plate whilst cooking the rest of our pancakes. Once done, stack your pancakes high and top with banana, blueberries and a tsp of almond butter - if you fancy!

BREAKFAST STUFFED MUSHROOMS

 Number of servings: 1   Preparation Time: 2 minutes   Cooking Time: 10 minutes

Breakfast doesn't have to be complicated, nor does it need to take more than 10 minutes to prepare. For us, breakfast (when we have it) has to be quick, nutritious and packed full of all the good stuff and this recipe certainly ticks all of those boxes. As well as that, the protein from the eggs will help keep you stay full and therefore, you're less likely to overeat and graze throughout the morning.

Whilst this recipe may scream simplicity, it certainly doesn't lack in flavour. In fact, the combination of ingredients works perfectly well together in creating a healthier version of our typical, grease filled and CARB boasting, English breakfast.

It should come as no surprise that the ultimate Super Fungi, the mushroom, manages to make its way onto my superfood list. It's quite obvious that our Primal ancestors consumed plenty of mushrooms in their existence and therefore, this makes them a perfect Primal ingredient.

Ingredients

2 portobello mushrooms
1 cup spinach
2 eggs
6 vine cherry tomatoes

Salt and pepper - to taste
Sprinkle parsley
1 tsp coconut oil

Method

Begin by heating a pan with 1 tsp coconut oil.

Once the coconut oil has melted, place your portobello mushrooms (stalk free) in the pan and lightly fry on both sides for a few minutes on medium heat.

Sprinkle your mushrooms with fresh parsley and salt and pepper to taste. Push the mushrooms to one side and crack both of your eggs in the pan and cook until done.

Whilst your eggs are cooking, set your plate up with a cup/handful of fresh spinach and a vine of cherry tomatoes.

Once your eggs are cooked, simply place them in the portobello mushrooms, pop them on your plate and serve up!

Mushroom caution

Because the skins of mushrooms are very delicate, try and always go for organic. Remember, it's impossible to just wash off pesticides from food.

SPINACH OMELETTE

🍴 Number of servings: 2　　🕐 Preparation Time: 5 minutes　　🕐 Cooking Time: 8 minutes

Ingredients

6 eggs

Coconut oil or ghee

Handful chopped spinach

Handful chopped fresh coriander

1/4 chopped onion

3 or 4 diced mushroom

1/4 of a cup of ham (or cooked bacon)

Herbs and spices (optional)

Handful grated cheese (optional)

Method

Heat the coconut oil or butter in a frying pan and toss in the diced spinach, mushroom, ham and onion.

Beat the eggs and add to the pan once the spinach has wilted. Heat gently and once it starts to cook, add your optional cheese, herbs and spices.

Using a spatula, carefully fold your omelette in half. Use the outside of the pan to form a nice half circle and continue to cook. If confident, try and flip it over so it cooks equally on both sides. Cook until brown on both sides.

Serving suggestions: Serve with salmon and avocado.

PRIMAL CEREAL

 Number of servings: 8   🕐 Preparation Time: 2 minutes

Ingredients

Coconut flakes (toasted see page 180)   Macadamias
6 tsp raisins   Cashews
6 tsp dried goji berries   Unsweetened almond milk or whole milk
Walnuts (see baking nuts on page 168)

Method

OK, so we know regular CARB loaded cereals are not allowed. Period! But how about replacing it with a truly wholesome Primal Cereal? You can purchase coconut flakes pre-toasted, but we prefer to make our own. You also don't need to cook the nuts, but again they are great if you prepare your own.

Just add as many nuts as you fancy, combine with the rest of the ingredients and serve with almond milk or grass fed, organic whole milk. We tend to make a batch and keep it in an airtight class jar in the cupboard. You can of course just make it up as you need it.

Drinks

METABOLISM BOOSTER COFFEE

🍴 Number of servings: 1   🕐 Preparation Time: 2 minutes

The Primal team all share a love for this Primal-approved coffee. It's an incredibly simple recipe but it's an amazing drink to start the morning with and hey, what's wrong with upgrading your morning coffee?

We find that this drink is a great way to help kick-start our metabolisms in the morning (whilst remaining in a fasted state). What's the secret to making your usual morning cup of coffee a metabolism booster? Coconut oil. That's right. Every morning we add a teaspoon of coconut oil to our morning coffee because it contains many health benefits.

To make this recipe our own (we can't really call adding a teaspoon of coconut oil to coffee our own recipe) we've also added an optional teaspoon of lucuma powder to truly make this a superfood morning cup of coffee. Plus, it tastes like caramel. Yum!

Ingredients

1 cup of coffee
1 tsp lucuma powder
1 tsp coconut oil

Method

Pour your usual morning coffee and add the lucuma powder and coconut oil. Stir and leave for a minute or two before drinking.

Primal on lucuma

Lucuma powder comes from the lucuma fruit and has a unique caramel flavour (truly it does). It contains iron, which can help reduce the feeling of tiredness and fatigue, as well as potassium and zinc, which are both important for supporting our nervous system and cognitive system.

Cocoa coffee

For possibly the nicest cup of coffee you are going to ever taste, that is full of healthy goodness, then add just 2 teaspoons of Virgin Cold Pressed Cocoa Butter. The flavour is awesome and it always reminds me of Christmas. Cocoa Butter is famed for slowing the signs of ageing, improving heart health and boosting our immune system.

SUPERFOOD HOT CHOCOLATE

🍴 Number of servings: 2   🕐 Preparation Time: 5 minutes

Just because you're living a Primal lifestyle it doesn't necessarily mean that you have to miss out on the finer things in life, especially when it comes to our favourite winter treats. So let us tell you, hot chocolate is definitely something you do not need to give up.

Thanks to this recipe you can make yourself a deliciously rich and dark hot chocolate drink – minus the CARBS and high sugar content! All you need are four ingredients and you'll soon find yourself in a soft blanket of hot chocolate goodness. You know one of the best things about Primal cooking? You can leave out the ingredients that provide you with nothing but empty calories and simply replace them with goodness.

Our Primal hot chocolate recipe isn't just your average mug of steamy, rich, hot chocolate. Instead, we've created a superfood hot chocolate that has a delicious combination of raw cacao, turmeric (a healing spice), cinnamon and almond milk that will keep you warm, satisfied and in top condition for the colder seasons.

Ingredients

2 cups almond milk or full fat milk
3 tsp raw cacao powder

1/8 tsp turmeric (any more and it will be too strong!)
1/4 tsp cinnamon

Method

Add all of your ingredients to a pan and mix until everything is combined.
Warm the pan and leave it to gently simmer for ten minutes until the flavours come out.
Pour into two mugs and serve!

FIBRE SHAKE

 Number of servings: 1   Preparation Time: 2 minutes

Ingredients

8g psyllium husk
20g WHEY protein powder
1 SlimShotz

1 tbsp of cold pressed coconut oil
or cocoa butter

Method

How important is fibre to our health? According to The American Journal of Clinical Nutrition – consuming 35g of fibre was associated with a lower risk of cardiovascular disease by as much as 54% and death from all causes by 37%.So basically we need to consume plenty of it.

I regularly start my day with my Fibre Shake. Even if I want to fast until my evening meal, I don't regard this shake as breaking my fast. The fibre is supplied from both psyllium husk and glucomannan (the only ingredient approved by the European Food Standards Agency to be able to claim that it helps to lose weight) which is the main ingredient in SlimShotz. I also add 20g of protein, and a tablespoon of coconut oil, that way I know I am starting my day in healthiest way possible.

Its dead simple to make. Simply add the 4 ingredients to a blender and blend for abut 20 seconds. That's all folks!

PRIMAL TEAS

🍴 Number of servings: 1   🕐 Preparation Time: 1 minute

Ingredients

1 herbal tea bag
Then add your favourite fresh flavours
Here are some of our favourites:
Slice of lemon
Piece of ginger
Lemongrass

Mint or peppermint
Slice of orange
Berries
Cinnamon stick
Coconut oil
Honey

Method

Tea is without doubt one of the healthiest drinks we can consume. Straight forward Green Tea is fantastic for its health benefits, but try and also drink a wide variety of different flavoured herbal teas. Why? Well, when you look at communities around the world that have high proportions of centenarians, drinking a wide variety of herbal teas throughout the years, is one of the few common traits.

Herbs are full of numerous phytonutrients and antioxidants that boost the immune system, acting as natural antibacterial and antiviral compounds. Their ability to protect us from free radicals and therefore certain cancers is well documented, as too is their ability to prevent symptoms associated with colds and flu.

Even when we drink herbal teas at Primal, we will often jazz them up with different fresh ingredients.

TURMERIC SLEEP SHOT

 Number of servings: 4   Preparation Time: 10 minutes

When it comes to sleep, I consider it to be one of the most important factors of our lives. Not only does sleep aid our body in its recovery from our daily activities, but it also helps protect our mental health, physical health and all in all, leads to a long and healthy, happy life.

If you've been struggling to sleep recently and have been feeling the knock-on effect then this Primal Turmeric Sleep Shot may just become your new best friend. I think we all know the value of getting a decent night's sleep but when we don't, the first thing we shouldn't be doing is running to the local chemist for a dose of sleeping pills. Instead, it's time to go back to basics with the amazing ingredients Mother Nature created for us.

This recipe is simple. Fact. It's made with 9 Primal-friendly ingredients, all of which our Primal ancestors would have used themselves. However, the two main stars of this recipe have to be turmeric and ginger - both of which provide our bodies with some pretty wonderful health benefits.

Let's start with turmeric. At its base, turmeric helps to reduce inflammation, lower your blood sugar levels, help the liver to detoxify, boosts your immune system, protects your digestive system and may help to reduce the risk of diabetes. All of these benefits can help promote better sleep quality and allows you to wake up feeling refreshed and rejuvenated.

When it comes to ginger, it's actually the root of the Zingiber officinale plant and is closely related to turmeric and cardamom. Ginger is well known for its calming effects and helps remove toxins from the body, promotes good gut health, reduces muscle soreness, promotes muscle recovery and contains anti-inflammatory properties. All of which, yup you guess it, helps promote a better night's sleep.

Ingredients

1 tbsp grated ginger
Pinch of black pepper
Pinch of fresh chilli
1 tbsp raw honey
1 1/2 cups coconut water
Juice of one lemon
1 tsp ground turmeric
60g grated carrot
1 tsp coconut oil

Primal on turmeric

Turmeric is one of the most powerful natural medicines we can add to our food. It is the richest source of the antioxidant substance known as curcumin.

I personally love to cook lots of dishes with this heaven-sent spice, but at the same time I still take a daily supplement to make sure I am not missing out on the goodness that it packs. After all, the spice is said to reduce the risk of prostate and skin cancer, brain tumours, leukemia, multiple sclerosis and depression. It's a natural painkiller that, for aches and pains in certain parts of the body, is said to be as effective as ibuprofen.

Method

In a blender add all of your ingredients and blend everything together until you have no large chunks. You should end up with 'bits' almost like fresh orange juice.

Once blended, pour the mixture into a large container to keep refrigerated and every evening, pour a shot's worth into a shot glass, throw it back and reap the benefits! Lately, I've been making this Turmeric Sleep Shot at the beginning of the week and enjoying a shot every evening an hour before bed.

These shots are best enjoyed cold and thrown back - bottoms up!

TIP: With this recipe, I like to focus on its benefits, rather than the taste. Whilst my Primal Turmeric Sleep Shot boasts a very sweet flavour, it does come with quite a kick of flavours. The best way to enjoy this health drink is with true shot style: throw it back and reap the benefits.

PRE-WORKOUT DRINK

Number of servings: 1   **Preparation Time: 2 minutes**

Ingredients

1 banana
1 cup coconut milk

1 *Primal Cure* Muscle 5x capsule (break in half and use the powder)

Method

Sometimes, just sometimes, we need that little extra boost of energy before a workout. With only 3 ingredients, it really is the quickest and most convenient pre-workout drink that you can make.

To make this the most effective pre-workout Primal drink, we've combined some of our best Primal fitness supplements with some well-nourished food ingredients.

Our muscle 5x includes five powerful ingredients to improve muscle function and to boost physical performance.

Simply pop all of your ingredients into a food blender and blend everything together until lump free. Enjoy 30 minutes to 1 hour before your workout.

POST-WORKOUT DRINK

🍴 Number of servings: 1   🕐 Preparation Time: 2 minutes

Ingredients

30g WHEY protein powder
1 cup almond milk or full-fat milk
1 date (to add sweetness)
1 banana

2 tsp fresh ginger
1 *Primal Cure* Creatine HIIT capsule (simply take the powder out)

Method

I'm bringing you one of my favourite post-workout protein drink recipes. Whether you're an athlete, a regular gym goer, or somebody just trying to keep active, what you consume after a workout is important. Think of your body as a car engine. During your workout, you're using the fuel to allow your body to max out and work hard. Once your workout comes to an end it's time to refuel, re-energise and re-hydrate to keep your engine going.

Simply pop all of your ingredients into a food blender and blitz until no bits are left. Pour into a glass/bottle and enjoy immediately post-workout.

COCONUT, BLUEBERRY AND LEMON AGUA FRESCA

 Number of servings: 2   Preparation Time: 10 minutes

Here is a Primal-friendly mocktail that's refreshing, light and full of ingredients that are good for you - not like your typical sugar loaded cocktail!

Whilst Agua Frescas are the perfect non-alcoholic drink, they can still be packed with sugar and artificial juices. Our coconut, blueberry and lemon Agua Fresca however, is made by the ingredients stated in the name of the drink. Therefore, you'll find no unnatural juices that are filled with extra sugar, no hidden ingredients and certainly no thickening agents.

For this recipe, you'll simply need four ingredients and a little ice, although the ice is optional. To make the drink you simply blend the coconut water with ice, a little raw honey and lemon and then pour the drink into a tall glass with frozen blueberries sitting at the bottom. We served ours with a lemon wedge for an extra kick. If you're after a refreshing drink this summer then this is definitely one to try! Plus, it's a great way to get the kids involved in a Primal lifestyle.

Ingredients

1/2 cup frozen blueberries
2 cups coconut water
2 cups ice cubes

1/4 tsp raw honey
6 tbsp lemon juice

Method

In a food processor add your frozen ice cubes, coconut water, raw honey and lemon juice and blend everything together until you get a crushed ice texture.

In two tall cocktail glasses, pop half of the frozen blueberries in each. Now pour the crushed coconut water on top of the blueberries and serve with a slice of lemon on each glass. Enjoy!

Primal on coconut water

If you're buying coconut water in a carton then please double check the ingredients as many companies like to add a little extra fructose which then makes the drink non Primal-friendly. Unadulterated coconut water however, is packed full of nutrients and minerals and offers numerous health benefits.

Main Meals

TURMERIC AND COCONUT FISH CURRY

🍴 Number of servings: 4   🕐 Preparation Time: 10 minutes   🕐 Cooking Time: 30 minutes

This quick and easy one-pan dish is packed full of delicious curry spices and provides our bodies with some pretty amazing anti-inflammatory benefits thanks to the turmeric and coconut. It's no secret that we're a big lover of both food ingredients at Primal Cure.

This dish is best served with a wedge of lime and lightly fried cauliflower rice.

Ingredients

PASTE
4 cloves garlic, peeled and diced
1 tsp fresh ginger, chopped
1 tbsp fresh turmeric (3 of *Primal Cure* Turmeric capsules)
2 tsp mustard seeds
1 tsp ground coriander
2 tsp cumin seeds
1 tbsp curry powder
1/2 tsp salt

OTHER
1 medium sweet red pepper, sliced
1 red onion
1 tbsp *Primal Cure* coconut oil
400ml full-fat coconut milk
1/2 sliced courgette
1 small bunch coriander (finely chopped)
600g mixed fish (we've used salmon, haddock and cod)
1 large cauliflower blitzed into rice
1 lime (sliced into wedges)
5 tenderstem broccoli sticks
Salt and pepper to taste

Method

Begin by making your red Thai curry paste.

Pop all of the ingredients into a food processor and blend until you have a creamy paste.

In a pan, pour in the creamy part of your coconut milk and bring to an almost boiling point (not for too long otherwise the milk will curdle) and then bring to the simmer.

Add the red Thai curry paste, red pepper, green beans, mangetout and fish sauce. Whilst this cooks, fry your beef in a separate pan until brown. Make sure not to overcook otherwise the meat will become tough.

Once brown, add the beef strips to the coconut milk, the rest of the coconut milk liquid and slowly stir. Leave on medium to low heat for 10-15 minutes for the flavours to soak into the meat. In the last 5 minutes, add your pineapple chunks.

Once done, serve and top with a sprinkle of fresh basil and a wedge of lime. Enjoy!

HEALTHY PUMPKIN CURRY SOUP

🍴 Number of servings: 6-8   🕐 Preparation Time: 10 minutes   🕐 Cooking Time: 30 minutes

Many people create pumpkin soup with double cream and whilst this ingredient can still be enjoyed as part of a Primal diet, we decided to experiment with coconut milk for extra health benefits.

This recipe was inspired by one of our favourite foods, curry. Thanks to the deliciousness of the pumpkin and the cream of the coconut milk, all the flavours work amazingly well together and the hint of curry powder is far from overpowering. If you're a big fan of curry (don't worry it's not spicy), then this will not disappoint.

You can either make this curry on the spot or make it in advance to allow the flavours to soak overnight. We much prefer option two but cooking it in the evening and serving up straight away is just as fine. Just make sure you allow it to simmer under a lid!

Ingredients

2 tbsp coconut oil
2x 400ml canned pumpkin purée
2 x 400ml canned full-fat coconut milk
1 cup vegetable stock (more if you prefer a less thick soup)
1 onion (diced)
6 garlic cloves crushed
2 tsp medium curry powder (or more if you desire)

1/2 tsp white pepper
1/2 oregano
1/2 tsp thyme
6 bacon medallions (cooked and cut into chunks)
1 pomegranate to serve (optional)
Pumpkin seeds to serve (optional)
Salt and pepper to taste

Method

Begin by heating a saucepan with coconut oil and adding the onion and garlic. Fry for 10 minutes on medium heat (or until the onion turns soft).

Add the pumpkin, bacon and spices and stir and cook for another 5 minutes. Add the coconut milk first and if the soup is a little too thick for your liking, then add the vegetable stock (mixed with water) and stir once again.

On low heat, leave the soup to simmer for 20 minutes. Once you're ready to serve, add salt and pepper to taste and serve with a tablespoon of pomegranate and pumpkin seeds.

Pumpkin in a can

Nowadays, for convenience, you can find natural canned pumpkin in your local supermarket. However, if you've got time on your hands and it's in season, then try making your own pumpkin purée by roasting the pumpkin, spooning out its flesh and whizzing it together in a food processor until you've created a purée.

RED THAI BEEF, COCONUT AND PINEAPPLE CURRY

 Number of servings: 3   Preparation Time: 10 minutes   Cooking Time: 20-25 minutes

Forget the nonsense packet red Thai curry pastes, we're going to show you how to make your very own fresh paste that's free from the sugar used in most shop brought sauces.

The secret to making the curry paste is down to the aromatics. We're talking onion, garlic, ginger and chilli. Whilst the ingredient list may seem a little large, it really does make a difference compared to the shop-bought stuff. You can certainly expect a more traditional Thai taste with this recipe, that's for sure.

As for the recipe itself, you can thank the full-fat coconut milk, colourful veg, juicy beef strips and the sweet pineapple for the finishing touch. These ingredients really do add lots of personality to the dish - not to mention flavour! Also, when it comes to the pineapple chunks, don't even think about opting for the tinned stuff! Grab a fresh, ripe pineapple and get chopping.

Red Thai curries are slightly different than other curries in the fact that they are more of a liquid texture. You have the coconut milk to thank for that - full-fat coconut milk of course.

Ingredients

RED THAI CURRY PASTE
1 small onion (diced)
1 red chilli (sliced)
2 garlic cloves (diced)
Juice of 1 lime
1 lemongrass stalk
1 tsp cumin
1 tsp ground coriander
1 tsp paprika
2 tbsp full-fat coconut milk (the cream)

CURRY
1 cup fresh pineapple chunks
350g lean cut beef strips
1 red pepper (sliced)
400ml full-fat coconut milk
100g mangetout
100g green beans
Handful of basil (chopped)
2 tbsp natural fish sauce
1 tbsp lime juice

Method

Begin by making your red Thai curry paste. Pop all of the ingredients into a food processor and blend until you have a creamy paste. In a pan, pour in the creamy part of your coconut milk and bring to an almost boiling point (not for too long otherwise the milk will curdle) and then bring to the simmer.

Add the red Thai curry paste, red pepper, green beans, mangetout and fish sauce. Whilst this cooks, fry your beef in a separate pan until brown. Make sure not to over cook otherwise the meat will become tough. Once brown, add the beef strips to the coconut milk, the rest of the coconut milk liquid and slowly stir. Leave on medium to low heat for 10-15 minutes for the flavours to soak into the meat. In the last 5 minutes, add your pineapple chunks. Once done, serve and top with a sprinkle of fresh basil and a wedge of lime. Enjoy!

Alternatives to beef

This curry works equally well with duck, lamb chicken or prawns. If you're vegetarian then add extra vegetables or experiment with tofu!

CAULIFLOWER AND BACON OMELETTE WITH BLACKBERRY SALAD

🍴 Number of servings: 4   🕐 Preparation Time: 10 minutes   🕐 Cooking Time: 15 minutes

We've used two delicious medallions of bacon in this recipe but if you're not a fan, or are simply looking to make this a vegetarian dish, then skip this ingredient.

When it comes to buying bacon, Steve and his family always tries to use organic and natural bacon medallions from their local butchers. If you are travelling, then in the supermarket, head for the meat counter and not the packaged food aisle. This way we know that it's coming from the right sources and that the food we're eating hasn't been processed, pumped or filled with other toxic ingredients.

Ingredients

1 tsp extra virgin olive oil for the pan
1 tbsp ghee
1 small cauliflower
2 bacon medallions
6 large eggs
1 tbsp chilli flakes
1 tbsp cumin seeds
2 tbsp flax seeds

100g grated gruyere cheese
Salt and pepper to taste (use quite a bit of pepper)

SALAD (mix everything together)
120g fresh salad leaves
1 tsp avocado oil
1 handful of blackberries

Method

Begin by preheating your oven to gas mark 4 (180 degrees Celsius) and oiling a non-stick pan with extra virgin olive oil.

Place your bacon medallions under a grill and cook on medium heat whilst you prep your omelette.

Cut your small cauliflower into florets and half lengthways. Once done, pop the cauliflower into the pan and heat on medium heat. Cook until slightly golden. Once golden, add 1 tablespoon of ghee to the pan and continue to cook until your cauliflower is soft. Once your cauliflower has cooked, add the cumin and flax seeds to the pan and fry for 1 minute (try not to burn them).

In a bowl, whisk together the eggs with the chilli flakes, salt and pepper. Add the grated cheese and bacon (cut into pieces) to the pan (covering evenly) and pour in your egg mix. Cook on medium heat until the base starts to firm up and then place the pan into the middle of the oven to cook for 15 minutes.

Once cooked, remove from the oven and leave to cool for a few minutes before serving with your blackberry salad.

Primal on cheese

Nowadays, cheese can have a bad rep in the media, but when eaten as naturally and organically as possible, it can be enjoyed in moderation as part of a Primal lifestyle. And when I say natural, I mean the kind that isn't stuffed in brightly coloured packaging or the orange squares added to burgers.

SMOKEY PORK MEXICAN BURRITO BOWL

Number of servings: 3 **Preparation Time: 10 minutes** **Cooking Time: 30 minutes**

Burrito bowls are becoming a popular dish and we thought that it would be a good idea to make a Primal-friendly one. This smokey pork Mexican burrito bowl is packed with the most delicious flavours and it works wonders with the burrito salad.

The idea of the burrito bowl is that it's an emptied burrito. Basically no tortilla! Takeaway burrito bowls are packed with CARBS and bad fats; however, we've simply ditched these by using cauliflower rice and lean cut pork.

This recipe isn't complicated at all. All it requires are a few ingredients, two essential spices – cumin seeds and smoked paprika – and roughly 40 minutes of your time. The best part about this dish is the smokey sauce that the pork cooks in. It's absolutely delicious and the flavour really compliments the rest of the salad. Pair your bowl with a fresh dollop of homemade guacamole (that only requires three ingredients) and you've got yourself a flavoursome Primal dish that's perfect for the whole family.

Ingredients

PORK
500g pork (diced)
2 tsp cumin seeds
2 tsp smoked paprika
1 pinch salt
1 pinch black pepper
3 cloves garlic finely chopped
1 tbsp extra virgin olive oil
1 large onion diced
2 medium red chillies)finely sliced
with no seeds)
1 large green pepper sliced
1 tin black beans
1 tin chopped tomatoes

1 tbsp apple cider vinegar organic
1 tsp tomato purée

BURRITO BOWL
2 medium cauliflowers grated into cauliflower rice
3 tbsp fermented red cabbage
15 vine cherry tomatoes (sliced)
3 large avocado mashed into a purée
3 tbsp lemon juice from a fresh lemon
3 tsp black pepper
2 medium limes sliced into wedges
3 cups mixed green leafs with spinach washed
3 tsp parsley (finely chopped)

Method

Begin by heating a large pan with oil. Add the pork to the pan and cook on medium heat until brown on all sides.

Add the cumin seeds, smoked paprika, salt, pepper, garlic, onion, red chilli and green pepper to the pan and cook for a few more minutes.

Add the chopped tomatoes, apple cider vinegar and drained black beans and mix everything together. Bring to the boil and then simmer for 30 minutes, adding the tomato purée halfway through before stirring and leaving to simmer for the remaining 15 minutes.

continued...

While your pork is cooking prepare your burrito bowl.

Evenly split the burrito bowl ingredients and add the cauliflower rice, cabbage, mixed salad and spinach and chopped tomatoes to sections of separate bowls. Leave space for the pork. E.g. three cups of spinach would be one cup per bowl.

Prepare the guacamole by adding a tbsp of lemon and pepper to the mashed avocado and mixing together. Set aside.

Once the pork has cooked completely and you have a thick sauce texture, add a portion to each bowl. Top the bowls with a tbsp of guacamole, a wedge of lime and sprinkle with parsley and more pepper (if you wish). Serve up and enjoy!

Primal Tip

Prep this meal in advance and have it as pre-made lunches/dinners. That way, the pork can really marinate in its sauce and you're left with a much more intense and smokey flavour.

FISH CAKES

🍴 Number of servings: 4   🕐 Preparation Time: 20 minutes   🕐 Cooking Time: 30 minutes

Ingredients

1lb/450g cod or similar white fish
1 cup coconut flour
1/2 cup chopped fresh coriander (dried if you don't have fresh)
1 spring onion (finely chopped)
2 or 3 tbsp red curry paste

2 tbsp fish sauce
1 egg (the white and the yolk)
3 green beans (finely diced) (optional)
1 tbsp lime juice
1 red onion (very finely diced)

Method

Chop up the fish, then add the fish and all the remaining ingredients into a blender.

Blend until it is nicely minced, but stop short of it becoming a purée (you may need to stop and start until you reach the correct consistency).

Put the mixture into a mixing bowl and pop in the fridge for an hour or two to firm up. On a baking tray, carefully shape the fish cakes with your hands (be careful not to over-handle them, else the fish will break off).

Optionally, coat in some primal batter before popping them in the oven (see page 186).

Then put in the oven on gas mark 4 (180 degrees Celsius), for around 30 minutes until the fish cakes are piping hot in the centre (this will vary based on the size of the fish cakes you have shaped).

Now make the chicken korma: Heat a pan with 1 tsp coconut oil. When hot, add the onion, garlic and ginger and fry until brown.

Add the cayenne pepper, garam masala, turmeric, cumin seeds and ground coriander to the pan.

Add the diced chicken to the pan and cook for 5 minutes on medium heat. Add the chicken stock and sultanas to the pan. Cover and simmer for 10 minutes (or until the chicken is thoroughly cooked and its juices run clear).

Whilst the chicken korma is simmering remove the top layer of parchment paper from your pizza (leaving the bottom) and slide the pizza onto a baking tray. Place the pizza into the middle of the oven and cook for 15 minutes (or until golden).

Once your chicken korma has cooked, add the greek yoghurt and stir until everything is mixed together. Cook for another 5 minutes.

Once your pizza is cooked, remove it from the oven and spoon the chicken korma on top. Serve with a fresh sprinkling of coriander and tuck in!

SEA BASS ASIAN STYLE

🍴 Number of servings: 2   🕐 Preparation Time: 10 minutes   🕐 Cooking Time: 10-15 minutes

Ingredients

2x 190g boneless fillet sea bass
1/2 chilli (finely chopped)
2 cloves garlic (finely diced)
1 tbsp raw honey
1 tsp ginger (minced)
1 tbsp fish sauce

2 tbsp coconut oil
1/2 stalk lemongrass (sliced diagonally)
Fresh coriander
Fresh lime

Method

Add the chilli, garlic, honey, ginger and lemongrass into a saucepan, pour in the fish sauce and coconut oil and cook gently.

After 5 minutes or so add the fish and cook as desired. If you like to leave the skin on (which is incredibly healthy), spend more time cooking with the skin in the oil. Once plated, cut the lime into 4 quarters, squeeze one quarter over each fish, and to make it look authentic serve the other on the plate. Sprinkle on the coriander and you're good to go.

Serving suggestions: Combine with Primal rice (page 191) or Primal mash (page 190) or with roast vegetables (page 189).

FIERY LENTIL AND SEED KEDGEREE

Number of servings: 4   **Preparation Time: 10 minutes**   **Cooking Time: 25 minutes**

The simple yet delicious Kedgeree dish is a recipe that has remained popular since the British Empire times and of course, draws inspiration from India. So how can we, while living a Primal lifestyle, still enjoy a dish that's well known for its grains? Well, like most of our recipes, we adapt it to suit our lifestyle. We simply get rid of the grains and replace them with Primal-friendly ingredients – such as lentils, cauliflower rice and chunky seeds.

Our take on the classic kedgeree dish is to dramatically reduce the number of CARBS. As well as that, this dish is full of healthy fats and nourishing, whole ingredients that your body will thank you for. The spice from the cayenne pepper also adds a nice heat to the kedgeree, which really complements the overall flavour. Although it's not overly spicy, however, if you're not a fan of spice then you can simply leave the cayenne pepper out and instead add a sprinkle of black pepper.

Ingredients

2 fillets smoked haddock
2 large eggs
1 tsp turmeric
1 tsp cayenne pepper
1 tsp coconut oil
250g cauliflower rice

250g cooked red lentils
1 tbsp mixed seeds
1/3 bunch coriander (finely sliced)
1 large onion diced
1 garlic clove (crushed)
Juice of 1/2 lemon

Method

Begin by grilling your smoked haddock fillets for 8-10 minutes.

In a saucepan, bring your eggs to boil for 8 minutes. Once done, drain the hot water and pop the eggs in a cold bowl to cool down before peeling.

In a pan, melt a tsp of coconut oil and add the chopped onion and garlic and fry until golden brown. Once done, add the spices and stir for a few minutes.

Add the cauliflower rice, lentils, mixed seeds and coriander. Carefully stir and whilst stirring, add the lemon juice.

Once everything is cooked, slice the boiled eggs and flake the haddock. Serve up the kedgeree and then top each plate with a fair serving of haddock and eggs. Top with more coriander if desired and serve.

Primal on lentils

Whilst lentils may be considered a carbohydrate, they're a natural and complex carbohydrate which is why they fall towards the bottom of the GI index. Again, if you read my book then you'll see that I've even included lentils in my 'top 40' list for all my vegetarian friends as they offer one of the richest levels of protein that you can get from a plant. Lentils are a very wholesome pulse, that contain a good amount of fibre, folate, iron, manganese, potassium, zinc, phosphorous, magnesium, copper, vitamin B1 (thiamin) and vitamin B6 (pantothenic acid).

CREAMY MUSHROOM AND BACON RISOTTO

 Number of servings: 4   Preparation Time: 5 minutes    Cooking Time: 25 minutes

If you thought that living a Primal lifestyle meant giving up your favourite creamy Italian dishes, then think again! My Primal mushroom and bacon risotto takes all the flavours of the traditional Italian dish and makes it the perfect Primal recipe that can be enjoyed by the whole family. Plus, you can whip this dish up in less than 30 minutes, which means no rumbling tummies!

This creamy mushroom risotto dish is well known and loved by many, including myself. However, the traditional recipe can be high in toxic fats and carbs which all in all, don't make for a very Primal meal. Therefore, to make this a dish that we can enjoy as part of our Primal lifestyle, I've made two simple changes. I've swapped the canned cream and butter for organic coconut milk and I've replaced the risotto for cauliflower rice. That's it. Thanks to these changes, you can now enjoy a creamy mushroom risotto that's grain-free, dairy-free and toxic-fat free.

Ingredients

250g sliced chestnut mushrooms
65g organic bacon (medallions)
3 tbsp coconut milk
1 medium diced onion
1/4 tsp sea salt
1 tsp low salt and sugar free soy sauce
1 tbsp coconut oil

2 garlic cloves chopped and diced
1/4 tsp black pepper
1 medium cauliflower blitzed into 'rice' (you can also use frozen cauliflower rice - just thaw it beforehand)
1 low salt vegetable stock
Parsley to garnish

Method

Begin by grilling your bacon medallions under the grill until crispy.

Whilst your bacon is cooking, heat a pan with 1 tablespoon of coconut oil until hot.

Add the onion, garlic and mushrooms and cook on medium heat for 5 minutes. Add the soy sauce, stir and cook for another minute or two.

Add the coconut milk, cauliflower rice and vegetable stock to the pan and mix everything together. Add the salt and pepper to the pan and leave to simmer for 15 minutes.

When everything is cooked through and has the texture of a creamy risotto, cut the crispy bacon up into bits and add them to the pan. Stir and serve. Garnish servings with fresh parsley.

Primal on mushrooms

For the past few thousand years, Eastern cultures have literally worshipped the famous fungi for its many health benefits. Mushrooms are rich in protein and come with a good dose of fibre too. They're also a powerful source of vitamins and minerals and help fulfil many deficiencies in our bodies when consumed regularly. Mushrooms promote stronger bones and a healthy immune system.

SMOKED CHICKEN BEAN STEW

 Number of servings: 4   Preparation Time: 10 minutes   Cooking Time: 70 minutes

Traditional smokey stew recipes often call for harissa paste which, most of the time, contains sugar and thickening agents. So in order to keep this recipe as Primal as possible, I've used two spices as an alternative. When mixed together, chilli flakes and caraway seeds can re-create a mild spicy harissa flavour. So much so that you won't notice the difference!

I've used organic chicken legs for this recipe but feel free to use the breast of the chicken if you prefer. As for the chorizo, make sure you go for organic chorizo that has reduced nitrates. My advice? Go to your local butchers. They'll be much healthier than your store-brought meat. If you can't find any Primal-friendly chorizo then go for organic bacon medallions.

Ingredients

1 tbsp extra virgin olive oil
4 chicken legs
170g organic chorizo (check the ingredients)
1 aubergine (sliced)
1 red pepper (sliced)
1 yellow pepper (sliced)
2 cups spinach
600g mixed beans (we used kidney beans, chickpeas and pinto beans)
400g tinned tomatoes
200g organic chicken stock (check ingredients for salt and sugar)
3 garlic cloves (crushed)
3 shallots (diced)
1 tbsp chilli flakes
1 tbsp caraway seeds
1 tsp smoked paprika

Method

Begin by preheating your oven to gas mark 4 (180 degrees Celsius). Heat a pan with olive oil and add the shallots and cook on medium heat until soft/golden brown. Add the garlic and cook for a further 2 minutes.

In a separate pan, add the chicken legs and chorizo and cook on medium heat until golden brown. The oil from the chorizo will be enough to provide your chicken with a lovely crispy coating.

Whilst your chicken cooks, add the peppers and spices to the garlic pan and cook on medium heat for 3-5 minutes. Add the tinned tomatoes, mixed beans and stir everything together. Finally, add the chicken stock, bring the pan to the boil and then leave to simmer for 5 minutes.

Once the chicken is golden, add everything to a crockpot and add the spinach. Stir, cover and pop in the middle of the oven to cook for 45 minutes or until piping hot. Once done, remove the pot from the oven (be careful it will be very hot) and serve.

Primal on chicken

If it's not both organic and free range don't buy it. Not just for the sake of our own health, but for the sake of the bird too. Only organic birds offer a clean source of protein and healthy fat.

Bell Peppers

The fabulously talented bell pepper (also known as capsicum) is indeed a truly Primal Superfood. In the main, it should be acknowledged for its high source of vitamin C, as a big yellow bell pepper has 341mg of it. That's roughly the same as five whole oranges!

One red bell pepper equates to three oranges and the green bell pepper, which is a little less sweet, still contains twice the vitamin C found in an orange.

Green peppers are in fact red bell peppers that have not yet ripened. As they ripen, they become sweeter and the vitamin C content increases. Orange and yellow varieties are specially bred to offer colour variety, and are also sweeter in taste.

Bell peppers aren't just about vitamin C, as just one pepper provides approximately 10% of our daily fibre requirements, plus they also contain vitamin A, vitamin B6, magnesium and potassium.

STUFFED RATATOUILLE PEPPERS

 Number of servings: 4   Preparation Time: 10 minutes   Cooking Time: 30 minutes

This recipe is great. A popular Paleo recipe, we'd have been fools not to be inspired by this dish. It's simple, quick to make, great to prep for the week ahead and can be made into a delicious lunch or dinner. Plus, thanks to its subtle spices, this dish is suitable for the whole family.

The grilled chicken used in this recipe is simply delicious and the flavouring works wonderfully well against the ratatouille. We've used a combination of spices - harissa, paprika and cumin - and it really does add that extra kick to the dish.

The best bit about this recipe is its simplicity (without neglecting its flavour). Simply chop up the required vegetables (or whatever you have in your fridge), coat it with a little flavouring and tinned tomatoes and chuck it in the oven to cook. Whilst that cooks, you can grill your chicken to perfection.

Ingredients

4 large peppers
1 large courgette
1 large aubergine
1 clover garlic crushed
225g cherry tomatoes
1 tin chopped tomatoes
Bunch chopped parsley
1 tbsp extra virgin olive oil
1 large red onion
Pinch salt and pepper

1 large avocado cut into chunks
1 handful parmesan cheese

GRILLED CHICKEN
350g chicken breasts diced
1 tsp cumin seeds
1/2 tsp smoked paprika
1 tbsp harissa

Method

Begin by preheating your oven to gas mark 4 (180 degrees Celsius).

Coat your chicken breasts with the Primal-friendly harissa sauce and then in a small bowl, mix together your cumin seeds and paprika and then sprinkle/coat over the chicken. Once done, place in the oven to cook for 25 minutes.

Prep your ratatouille by cutting all your vegetables (minus the avocado) into chunks. Grab a tray and pop your cut up vegetables on top. Drizzle with the olive oil and chopped tomatoes. Finish by flavouring the veg with a little pepper and salt. Once done, pop this in the oven beside your chicken and leave to cook for 30 minutes.

Whilst your chicken and veg are cooking, slice your bell peppers in half, de-seed them and then pop them on a baking tray. When you have 5 minutes left of cooking time for your ratatouille, pop the bell peppers in the oven to soften and remove the chicken.

Once your five minutes is up, remove everything from the oven. Cut your chicken into chunks and add the avocado to your ratatouille. Stuff the vegetables and chicken into your bell peppers.

Finish by sprinkling with a little extra seasoning and some parmesan cheese (or cheese of choice).

Vegetarian option

Whilst this recipe contains some meat from the grilled chicken, please do feel free to replace it with tofu or another high protein ingredient. To make it vegan-friendly, you'll need to get rid of the cheese!

PRIMAL SPAGHETTI BOLOGNESE

 Number of servings: 6 · Preparation Time: 5 minutes · Cooking Time: 25 minutes

A family favourite is spaghetti bolognese. It's rich, warming and incredibly easy to make during the week when we're strapped for time.

Whilst this recipe may differ a little from the classic recipe (no CARBS), it certainly still delivers flavour, taste and the most important element: comfort. The pairing of the bolognese works wonderfully against the carrots and courgette. The carrots add a nice 'whole' texture to the dish and their subtle sweetness pairs brilliantly with the mince and its sauce.

Another important factor about making this recipe Primal-friendly is to use beef mince that's organic and grass fed. We can't stress enough how important this is. On top of that, we'll be making our own sauce (which you'll do every time from now on, once you see how easy it is) so we know exactly what we're putting into our body.

Not only is this recipe a good source of protein, vitamins and minerals, but the volume from the courgette and carrots will also leave you feeling fuller for longer. We hope you enjoy our Primal take on the classic spaghetti bolognese recipe. The bolognese sauce is everything a bolognese sauce should be. As the Italians would say... Perfecto!

Ingredients

500g lean mince meat
2 tins chopped tomatoes
1 cup mushrooms sliced
2 garlic cloves (grated)
1 large onion (diced)
1 tbsp tomato purée

500 grams mix of carrot and courgette (spiralized)
1 tsp rosemary
1 tbsp chopped fresh basil
1 tbsp dried oregano
2 bay leaves
Salt and pepper to taste

Method

Heat a pan with a little oil and add your diced onion, garlic, mushrooms, rosemary and oregano and fry for a few minutes until your onion starts to brown.

Add the mince meat to the pan and cook until brown.

Add the two tins of chopped tomatoes and bring to the boil. Add your bay leaves and fresh basil and bring to the simmer for 15-20 minutes.

Whilst your mince cooks, spiralize your carrots and courgette. Just before you serve them you'll want to pop them in the microwave for a minute or two. Cooking them fully will simply make them soggy.

5 minutes before your mince is cooked, add the tomato purée and salt and pepper to the dish to taste.

Once cooked, serve your spiralized veg on a plate and top with the bolognese. Add an extra sprinkle of fresh basil if you wish and serve up!

CRISPY GLAZED ORANGE SALMON WITH STICKY AUBERGINE

Number of servings: 2   **Preparation Time: 10 minutes**   **Cooking Time: 40 minutes**

We love salmon. It's a brilliantly high omega 3 fish that's packed full of nourishing health benefits. Our favourite way to cook salmon is to pan fry it for a crispy, flavoursome finish and recently, we've experimented a little with a marinade that sparks a brilliantly sweet flavour.

Like most of our dishes, this recipe is incredibly simple to whip up (if prepared in advance) which means it certainly makes for a great weekday dish. The pairing of the salmon and aubergine also works incredibly well. Finish it off with a side of veg (we've used a stir fry veg mix) and you've got yourself a healthy and hearty dish that's full of all the good stuff - including the good fats and protein!

Ingredients

SALMON
1/4 cup juice from half an orange
1 clove garlic (grated)
2 salmon fillets
1 tbsp honey
1 tbsp extra virgin olive oil
1 tsp chilli flakes (optional)

AUBERGINE
2 tbsp soy sauce reduced salt and sugar
1 tbsp honey
1 tbsp extra virgin olive oil

VEG
220g veg mixed green veg works the best!

Begin by preheating your oven to gas mark 4 (180 degrees Celsius).

In a bag, add your salmon fillets and the ingredients for the salmon and shake well. Pop the bag into the fridge to marinate for a few hours/overnight.

When you're ready to prep your meal, slice your aubergine in half and score it with crisscrosses. In a bowl, mix together the aubergine sauce and then cover the two aubergine slices. Pop them onto a tray with foil and cook for 30 minutes in the oven. After 30 minutes remove from the oven and set aside.

Heat a pan with extra virgin olive oil (make sure it's very hot) and then bring to medium heat. Add your salmon fillets, drizzle the rest of the marinade from the bag over them and cook on medium heat. After 10 minutes, flip both fillets onto the other side and continue to cook until soft pink.

Whilst the salmon fillets fry in the pan, cook the green veg by boiling or frying the veg and leave to simmer (once cooked) until the salmon and aubergine are ready to serve.

When you have just 5 minutes left of cooking the salmon, add the aubergines to the pan and fry them until you get a charred topping.

Once the salmon and aubergine are fully cooked, serve them up with the veg, sprinkle with pepper and tuck in!

Cooking tip

Let the marinade soak into the salmon for a few hours (overnight would be even better) as this really boosts the flavour of the dish.

Get the kids involved

Get them to help with the marinade and shake the bag around. We always find that when we get the kids involved, it helps to ease them into new flavours, textures and foods!

CRANBERRY SPROUTS WITH SWEET AND SALTED ROASTED NUTS

Number of servings: 6 | Preparation Time: 5 minutes | Cooking Time: 40 minutes

---

For this dish, we've taken the traditional Christmas sprouts and bumped them up a little. Not only does it make them more appealing but they can also be enjoyed all year round.

We love sprouts and they're packed full of incredible vitamins and minerals. If cooked properly (not overly done), your body will love you for consuming them too. Due to their multitude of health benefits, we believe sprouts should be at the top of every family's vegetable list. If they don't usually rock your boat then this dish manages to take away the strong taste of the sprouts and instead, creates a lovely sweet and salty flavour that works wonderfully well with the cranberries.

As well as its flavour, another thing that we love about this recipe is how incredibly easy it is to make. All you need is a roasting pan and the required ingredients and then all you have to do is shake the ingredients together in the pan, pop in the oven and roast for 30-40 minutes.

Ingredients

3 cups peeled brussel sprouts
1 tbsp extra virgin olive oil
1/4 tsp salt
Black pepper (as much as you like!)

1 1/2 cups mixed nuts or nuts of your choice
1 tbsp fruit syrup (refined and sugar-free with no artificial sweeteners)
1 cup cranberries

Method

Begin by preheating your oven to gas mark 5 (190 degrees Celsius).

Oil a roasting tray and pour your ingredients in and mix around until everything is covered in the oil and syrup.

Pop the tray in the middle of the oven and roast for 30-40 minutes.

Check your brussel sprouts are golden, crisp and soft. Once done, remove your dish from the oven and serve up! You can also add extra fresh cranberries for an added touch of sweetness.

Primal on sprouts

Sprouts increase the production of proteolytic enzymes. These make the digestion of both carbohydrates and proteins a lot easier. Sprouts are also known for boosting our metabolism, alkalising the body and helping to prevent both cancer and heart disease.

SWEET CHILLI AND LEMON ASIAN PORK

🍴 Number of servings: 4　　🕐 Preparation Time: 10-15 minutes　　🕐 Cooking Time: 12-15 minutes

There's nothing we love more than creating simple recipes with basic ingredients that deliver incredible flavours with minimal effort. With that said, our sweet chilli and lemon Asian pork recipe is all of those things.

We love oriental foods and just because we believe in a Primal lifestyle, it doesn't mean that you'll find us giving up our favourite foods. Instead, we simply put our own twist to it and make it Primal-friendly.

So, thanks to our Primal-friendly version, this sweet chilli and lemon Asian pork is deliciously tender, sweet, slightly spicy and packed with the right amount of garlic and spring onions. However, this recipe wouldn't be one of our favourites if it didn't have our easy homemade sweet chilli sauce. Once you make this, you'll never look at store bought sauces again! Not only is it healthy, but it contains the most natural Primal ingredients. While making your own sauce may sound like a lot of effort, it really isn't! In 5 minutes you'll have the most amazing fresh sweet chilli sauce you could ask for.

Ingredients

400g pork strips (or diced)
1 tbsp coconut oil
1 whole lemon - juice
2 tsp sugar free fish sauce
Primal sweet chilli sauce
2 spring onions (sliced)
1 cup of nuts (chopped)
2 tbsp fresh coriander (chopped)
4 lettuce leaves

SWEET CHILLI SAUCE

1 tbsp apple cider vinegar
3 tbsp water
1 tsp fresh red chilli (finely diced)
2 tbsp fresh garlic (diced/minced)
2 tbsp raw honey
1 tsp fresh ginger (grated)
1/4 tsp himalayian salt

Method

Begin by heating a pan with 1 tbsp coconut oil.

Once the pan is hot, add the pork and cook on medium heat until done.

Whilst the pork cooks, make the sweet chilli sauce. Add all of the ingredients to a bowl, mix together and set aside.

In another bowl, add the lemon juice and fish sauce and mix together. Add the spring onions, mixed nuts and fresh coriander. Mix once more.

Once the pork has cooked, remove from the pan and leave to cool and rinse under hot or cold water.

Add the pork to the lemon sauce and mix until the sauce covers the pork. Add the sweet chilli sauce and mix everything together. We'd advise slowly adding the sweet chilli sauce and tasting as you go. You may not need all of it.

Serve your pork in lettuce wraps and enjoy!

Primal tip

If you can, buy organic pork and organic raw honey. Both ingredients are much healthier for us, and this way, we'll know exactly what we're consuming!

HEALTHY CHICKEN FRIED AVOCADO RICE

Number of servings: 4   **Preparation Time: 10 minutes**   **Cooking Time: 15 minutes**

This recipe is definitely a cheat from the classic Chinese chicken fried rice. Of course, the original recipe is packed full of fat and CARBS, but our recipe reduces the amount of both by using healthier choices such as cauliflower rice, a touch of extra virgin olive oil (instead of vegetable oil which is abundant in Chinese cooking) and a healthy dose of avocado.

I'll be honest. We weren't completely confident about how well this recipe would turn out. Could we really whip up a Primal-friendly recipe that replicated the taste of a very popular Chinese takeout dish? Well yes, apparently we could!

We also love the addition of the avocado in this dish. It's a little different but the avocado and the protein of the chicken will really leave you feeling satisfied after.

Ingredients

1 cauliflower head blitzed in a food processor until crumbly
3 regular chicken breasts (cooked and diced)
2 tbsp spring onions
1 small white onion diced
1 tbsp extra virgin olive oil

1 tsp soy sauce (low sugar and low salt)
2 large eggs (beaten)
1 red bell pepper
1 large avocado (cubed)
1 cup frozen peas
1/4 tsp salt
Sprinkle pepper

Method

First, thoroughly cook the 3 chicken breasts until their juices run clear.

In a pan/wok add together the oil and soy sauce and fry over medium heat. Add the onion and spring onions and mix together with the sauce and cook for a further 5 minutes until the onion has browned.

Add the rice, pepper, chicken and frozen peas and mix together with the onions and sauce. Cook for 5 minutes before moving all ingredients to the side of the pan and adding the eggs and mixing together with the rest of the ingredients whilst they cook.

Cook for a few more minutes before adding the avocado and then serve up.

HEALTHY FISH BOWL CHOWDER

Number of servings: 4 **Preparation Time: 5 minutes** **Cooking Time: 25 minutes**

If you love fish then you'll love this recipe! We've managed to take your classic fish chowder and turn it into something that's not only Primal-friendly but low in sugar and CARBS too. You can add whatever fish you like to the dish. Whether it's cod, salmon, prawns or squid, just go with what you fancy! The great thing about fish is the amazing benefits it has for our body and overall health.

Whilst you can make the dish with just one fish, it takes on a whole different flavoursome dimension when you combine multiple fishes such as salmon, cod, haddock, prawns and squid. The different flavours from each fish allow the fish bowl chowder to work its magic on your taste buds. It's a great low calorie and high protein dish and works well paired with bright vegetables.

Give this healthy fish bowl chowder recipe a go for your next meal if you're after something a little different and warming. You'll have it whipped up within 30 minutes and eaten in 5!

Ingredients

390g fish pie mix
150g prawns
80g squid
1/2 can chopped tomatoes
400g fish stock
1/2 onion (diced)

2 garlic cloves (minced)
1 lemon (sliced)
300g stir-fry mix - peppers, cabbage, carrot, bean sprouts and broccoli
2 tbsp extra virgin olive oil

Method

In a pan heat 1 tbsp olive oil, add the onion and garlic and fry until brown.

Add the fish, squid and prawns and cook for a few minutes. Add the chopped tomatoes and fish stock and bring to the boil. Once boiled, reduce heat to a simmer and cook for 10-15 minutes (or until the fish is done).

In a separate pan, add 1 tbsp olive oil and heat. Add the stir-fry mix and cook for 5-7 minutes. Serve in a separate bowl.

Once your chowder has cooked, pour into bowls and serve with a wedge of lemon. Enjoy!

HARISSA SPICED CHICKEN TRAYBAKE

🍴 Number of servings: 4   🕐 Preparation Time: 10 minutes   🕐 Cooking Time: 45-60 minutes

The harissa paste in this recipe is very Primal-friendly. For those of you who are new to harissa paste – it's a spicy red condiment that can be used within many recipes. It certainly adds a kick to any dish (but not too overpowering). To make your own you need to blend chillies into a thick paste with garlic, extra virgin olive oil and aromatic spices. We like to use cumin, caraway and coriander. You can even add red peppers, tomatoes and lemon to make it a little bit bulkier. We've also used this harissa paste in our Smoked Chicken Bean Stew (page 118) and Stuffed Ratatouille Peppers (page 122), if you want to remind yourself of the combination used.

Our two favourite ingredients for this traybake recipe are the chicken and cherry vine tomatoes.

A lot of people tend to think that eating healthily means restriction and tons of rabbit food (aka, salads and nuts), and whilst salads and nuts are full of amazing ingredients, they can tend to get a little repetitive. Remember, our ancestral forefathers benefited from a very diverse diet.

Ingredients

6 chicken thighs
1 pack cherry vine tomatoes
1 lemon - wedges
1 garlic bulb - diced/crushed
100g butternut squash - wedges
2 cups fresh spinach
1 tsp extra virgin olive oil - for the spinach dressing

Sprinkle salt and pepper - for the spinach dressing
3 tbsp harissa paste - Primal-friendly
1 tbsp extra virgin olive oil
6 tenderstem broccoli stalks
Sprinkle salt and pepper (to taste)
1 tbsp cumin seeds
1 large pepper - or mixed slices
1/3 tinned tomatoes

Method

Begin by preheating your oven to gas mark 5 (190 degrees Celsius). Oil a roasting tray with 1 tbsp extra virgin olive oil.

Score lines across each chicken thigh and then rub the Harissa paste over them - covering them evenly. Sprinkle with pepper, salt and cumin and then place them in the roasting tray.

Scatter the garlic and other ingredients (excluding the vine tomatoes) around the chicken. Squeeze the lemon wedges all over the ingredients and then add the squeezed wedges into the tray and place the vine tomatoes on top.

Lightly toss and shake your roasting tray and then pop in the middle of the oven to roast for 45 minutes - 1 hour (until the chicken thighs are cooked and crispy). Once cooked, serve your Harissa spiced chicken traybake with a side of fresh spinach tossed with 1 tsp extra virgin olive oil. Enjoy!

Supermarket caution

If you do buy your Harissa paste from the supermarket, always check the ingredients on the back of the box. Some can be natural with just the spices, whilst others can be packed full of sugar and other non-Primal nasty ingredients!

LAMB HOT POT

Number of servings: 4 • **Preparation Time: 20 minutes** • **Cooking Time: 2-4 hours**

Lamb is an excellent source of protein and Omega-3 fatty acids. It's rich in minerals such as zinc, iron, selenium, phosphorus, potassium, copper and magnesium, plus it's a great source of vitamin B12, vitamin B3 (niacin), vitamin B2 (riboflavin), vitamin B6 and B5 (pantothenic acid). Both lamb and beef are regarded as red meats.

Red meat is a great source of iron. If you feel that you are lacking in it, then adding a few lamb dishes to your weekly line up of meals should prove beneficial.

Lamb is rich in zinc, which among other things provides a boost to our immune system. From some farms, depending on the pasture (and I am assuming of course that we are only buying organic) lamb can actually provide more Omega-3 per gram than beef. It also contains conjugated linoleic acid (CLA), which in some research studies has been shown to fight off breast cancer.

Ingredients

Lean lamb (600g diced or half leg joint)
Lamb stock (300ml) (low salt and organic)
25g almond flour (or 35g for thicker sauce)
1/2 bottle red wine (optional)
1/2 cauliflower (separated into florets)

3 cloves garlic (finely diced or crushed)
200g of button mushrooms
3 leeks (finely sliced)
4 carrots (sliced)
3 tbsp tomato purée
Fresh thyme
Fresh rosemary
Salt and pepper

Method

Put the wine, lamb stock (I like to make the stock a little thicker than normal), almond flour and tomato purée in a pot and slowly bring to the boil while stirring. If you don't want to use wine, then increase the stock to about 500ml.

Then, put all the vegetables, herbs and lamb into a big roasting pot and pour over the stock. If it doesn't cover everything, then you will need to make and add more stock.

Add a pinch of salt and pepper and cook in the oven on a low heat (gas mark 2/150 degrees Celsius) until the meat is really tender.

SALMON, BROCCOLI AND SPINACH FRITTATA

 Number of servings: 4   Preparation Time: 10 minutes    Cooking Time: 20 minutes

Whilst this recipe is quick, it really is a true crowd pleaser. Of course, you can find loads of frittata recipes on the internet but this is our Primal favourite.

The flavours from the salmon and the egg really help to engross our taste buds and honestly, this salmon, broccoli and spinach frittata can be enjoyed whatever time of the day – morning, lunch or dinner! It really is a quick and easy recipe, packed with protein, healthy fats, vitamins and minerals!

You can choose to serve this frittata with a crunchy side salad (try adding some sauerkraut) or with some delicious greens. Our favourite would be the salad option!

Ingredients

1 tbsp thyme
2 salmon fillets
1 handful tenderstem broccoli
1 handful spinach

1 tbsp extra virgin olive oil
Sprinkle salt and pepper
1/4 cup garden peas
6 medium eggs

Method

Begin by frying your salmon fillets in a large pan with olive oil and thyme until both fillets are cooked (but not overdone).

Once your salmon fillets are done, tear them into tiny chunks and place them on a plate to one side.

In the same pan (using the same oil from the salmon) fry the peas and broccoli for a few minutes.

In a bowl, whisk together your eggs with some salt and pepper and then pour the mixture into your pan on medium heat. Top with the spinach and salmon chunks. Cook for 5 minutes and then transfer your pan under a grill and cook for another 5 minutes (or until done).

Once cooked, serve up with a side of salad/veg - enjoy!

CHILLI STUFFED PUMPKIN

 Number of servings: 4  Preparation Time: 5 minutes  Cooking Time: 1 hour 30 minutes

This recipe is incredibly easy to create and it certainly has a Mexican punch to it.

We've taken an unusual twist on the classic chilli con carne and paired it with a deliciously sweet roasted pumpkin. The two actually work amazingly well together flavour wise - plus it's a great way to get the kids to eat healthy too.

Ingredients

500g minced beef
400g tinned chopped tomatoes
400g kidney beans (drained)
1 tbsp chilli powder
1 clove garlic
1 tbsp paprika
1 tbsp cayenne pepper

1 tbsp cumin
1/2 onion (diced)
2 culinary pumpkins
Sprinkle of pepper
Pinch of salt
Sprinkle parsley (for topping)

Method

Begin by preheating your oven to gas mark 6 (200 degrees Celsius).

Once warm, place your pumpkins in the middle of the oven and cook for 40-60 minutes (dependant on your choice of softness).

Halfway through roasting your pumpkins, you can start to make your chilli. Begin by cooking your mince and onion in a pan on high heat until the mince has browned.

Once cooked, add your tin of chopped tomatoes, spices and garlic and then stir together and bring to the boil.

Whilst your chilli is cooking, remove your pumpkins from the oven (if cooked), slice them in half and leave to cool. Once cool, remove the insides from the pumpkins and prepare them to be stuffed.

Once boiled, bring to simmer and cook for another 15-20 minutes. Once cooked, add your drained kidney beans and cook for a further 5 minutes.

When your chilli is cooked, simply scoop a portion into the 4 halves of the pumpkins. Top with some fresh parsley and serve whilst hot!

Vegetarian option

If, however, you're not a meat eater then you can simply miss out the beef completely and add a few more kidney beans to the dish for some extra protein! Either way, this recipe is full of Primal-friendly ingredients and, hopefully, will become a staple in your family meals.

Primal on pumpkin

Pumpkin is actually a great vegetable to get creative in the kitchen with. It's a good source of Vitamin E (Alpha Tocopherol), Thiamin, Niacin, Vitamin B6, Folate, Iron, Magnesium and Phosphorus as well as Dietary Fibre, Vitamin A, Vitamin C, Riboflavin, Potassium, Copper and Manganese.

BANG BANG CHICKEN

 Number of servings: 2    Preparation Time: 5 minutes    Cooking Time: 20 minutes

If you're feeling a little blue for some weekday meal inspiration then look no further than our delicious bang bang chicken recipe. It's simple, mouthwatering and full of healthy fats and essential protein.

The chicken itself is actually coated with peanut butter (all natural) and is mixed with lime, a little hint of chilli and whole milk. It may sound like an unusual combination but trust us, this dish is packed full of flavouring that will leave you wanting for more.

We've topped our bang bang chicken with an added sprinkle of peanuts but this is optional. Other than that, the peanut butter coating does all the talking for this recipe. Pair it with some simple lettuce wraps and you've got yourself a Primal-friendly dish that is perfect for the whole family!

Ingredients

1 tsp coconut oil
2 diced chicken breast - or shredded chicken (enough for two)
2 tbsp natural peanut butter (we use meridian peanut butter)
1 tbsp lime juice
1 tsp chilli flakes
2 tbsp whole milk

1 tbsp soy sauce or coconut aminos (if you cannot find Primal-friendly)
4 lettuce leaves
1/3 sliced cucumber
Handful peanuts (optional - for topping)
4 slices lime
1/4 grated carrot

Method

Begin by heating a pan with 1 tsp coconut oil.

Once your pan is hot, add the diced chicken breast and cook until done.

In a bowl, add the peanut butter, milk, lime, chilli flakes and soy sauce/coconut aminos and mix well. Once mixed, add your cooked chicken and stir until the sauce is covering the chicken completely.

Add your chicken to the lettuce wraps and top with cucumber, sliced carrots and extra lime wedges (optional).

Tuck in and enjoy!

PRIMAL BURGERS

🍴 Number of servings: 2-3　　🕐 Preparation Time: 10 minutes　　🕐 Cooking Time: 15 minutes

Ingredients

450g lean mincemeat (beef, pork or lamb)
1 onion (finely chopped)
1 egg (pre-whipped or blended)

Salt and pepper
Herbs (3 or 4 tbsp, we suggest smoked paprika, chilli, tarragon, coriander or cumin)

Method

In a blender, gently pulse the meat with the onions, salt, pepper and egg and add your favourite herbs.

Try and avoid it becoming a purée, some texture is always best.

As their flavours generally become diluted during cooking, we find that you normally require more herbs than you first think.

On a chopping board, shape the burgers with your hands, then you can either shallow fry in coconut oil, butter, ghee or place in the oven. If frying, fry on a medium heat for about 4 minutes each side for medium, longer if you prefer well done, or about 20 minutes in the oven at gas mark 7 (220 degrees Celsius).

HUNTER / SHEPHERD'S PIE

Number of servings: 4   Preparation Time: 15 minutes   Cooking Time: 30 minutes

Ingredients

Cauliflower mash (see page 190)
500g lean mincemeat (beef, pork or lamb)
2 cloves garlic (finely diced)
2 sticks celery (finely diced)
1 or 2 carrots (finely diced)

1 large onion (finely diced)
3 tbsp tomato purée
2 tbsp smoked paprika
Herbs (your favourites, fresh or dried)
Salt and pepper
Butter (unsalted)

Method

Heat the butter in a pan and toss in your garlic, carrots, celery, onion and mincemeat and cook until the meat has browned.

Now it's time to place in your favourite herbs (I like to add thyme), tomato purée with a little salt and pepper and stir for a further 4 or 5 minutes.

Put the mixture into a clear oven dish (always looks better when serving if your friends can see your creation) and spread the cauliflower mash over the top. Cook for around 20 to 30 minutes in the oven at gas mark 4 (180 degrees Celsius) until the cauliflower starts to brown.
Once finished place some chopped herbs on the top and serve.

LOW CARB PAD THAI PRAWN AND PEANUT NOODLES

🍴 Number of servings: 2   🕐 Preparation Time: 15 minutes   🕐 Cooking Time: 10 minutes

Creamy, nutty, hearty and nutritious, this is a recipe you'll not want to miss. Think you had to say goodbye to your beloved noodle dishes? Think again! Thanks to the wonderful Sharitaki noodles, also known as 'miracle noodles,' you can enjoy a Primal-friendly dish that tastes almost like your favourite Thai takeout dish!

Shirataki noodles are thin, translucent and traditional Japanese noodles that are made from the konjac yam. They're largely made out of water and glucomannan (a water-soluble dietary fibre) and are very low in digestible CARBS and calories. We'll admit that they don't have much flavour if consumed on their own, but once covered with our delicious nutty sauce, you'll never notice their plain flavour.

Consider this dish to be a quick midweek turn around. Many people think that Thai dishes have to be complicated and full of various ingredients. However, we've proved that they can, in fact, be pretty easy and enjoyable to make.

We loved experimenting with the sauce for this recipe and in true Thai style, we decided on a nutty peanut sauce made with nutritious and Primal-friendly ingredients. Peanuts are rich in essential nutrients such as fibre, protein, minerals and healthy fats. They also contain plenty of antioxidants and provide our bodies with many health benefits. What's not to love? A Thai dish that's hearty, creamy and tastes almost like the real deal. Perfect!

Ingredients

2 servings shirataki noodles
1 pinch Himalayan salt
1 tbsp Primal coconut oil
10-14 large king prawns
2 cloves garlic diced
1 egg
115g bean sprouts

2 tbsp chives
1/2 cup natural peanut butter
2 tbsp fish sauce
4 tbsp water
1 tsp raw honey
1 tbsp and 1 tsp chilli flakes
1 lime (cut into wedges for serving)

Begin by making the sauce. Add the peanut butter, chilli flakes, fish sauce, water, honey, garlic and 1 tbsp chives to a bowl and mix together. Taste and adjust by adding additional water/honey/chilli flakes.

Heat a frying pan with 1 tbsp coconut oil over medium heat. Add the prawns with the salt and cook until just pink on the outside (this should take 2-4 minutes). You don't want to overcook the prawns. Add the drained noodles, stir and create a well in the middle. Crack the egg in the middle of the well and scramble until fully cooked.

Add the sauce to the noodles and mix until combined. Take the pan off the heat and add the bean sprouts and remaining chives. Squeeze juice from the lime and serve with an additional wedge of lime if desired.

Primal tip

Sharitaki noodles can be found in most supermarkets; however, they're often re-named as 'low-calorie noodles'. It's best to check the ingredients or shop online!

Lose weight

Shartitaki noodles are made from glucomananan, which is the only ingredient recognised by the European Food Standards Agency to aid weight loss.

CHICKEN, CHICKPEA AND SWEET MANGO PRIMAL CURRY

🍴 Number of servings: 4   🕐 Preparation Time: 20 minutes   🕐 Cooking Time: 20 minutes

There's something about homemade curries that always leaves me coming back for more. The flavour, the colour, the warmth and the different ingredients. I absolutely love getting in the kitchen with my family and creating dishes that are not only good for the body, but good for the soul too. When I say 'soul' what I really mean is creating a dish that provides you with joy when you get in the kitchen – seeking pleasure out of the food you're cooking for your family. That's what cooking delicious food should be about, right?

This chicken, chickpea and sweet mango primal curry a family favourite. It's a delicious combination of sweet and spicy (just a hint) and has a lovely amount of creaminess – thanks to the coconut milk. Coconut milk, unlike cow's milk, is completely lactose free, which also makes this a dairy free curry. While Primal Cure is not anti-organic cow's milk, coconut milk is definitely more beneficial to our overall health.

Personally, I believe this curry is everything a curry should be. It's full of flavour, comforting and nourishing. Pair it with some cauliflower rice and you've got the perfect Primal dinner.

Who says you can't have a curry that's not only delicious but good for you too? Not me! Go on, give this one a go.

Ingredients

1 tbsp extra virgin olive oil
1 tbsp cumin seeds
3/4 tsp chilli flakes
2 tsp turmeric
Handful of fresh coriander
1 1/2 tsp ginger peel
2 cloves garlic
1 large mango (ripe but not overly ripe)
1 can chickpeas

1 can chopped tomatoes
1 can coconut milk (full fat)
1 bag spinach
2 chicken breasts (cooked)
3 chicken thighs (cooked)
1 medium onion (diced)
1 cauliflower head blitzed into rice
Pepper to taste
1/4 tsp salt

Method

Begin by heating a large pan with extra virgin olive oil. Heat until hot and then add the cumin seeds and toast them for a few minutes. Be careful not to burn them!

Add the onions and cook until brown. Add the ginger, garlic, chilli flakes, coriander and turmeric then leave to cook for a few more minutes whilst stirring.

Add the cooked chicken, chickpeas, tin of tomatoes and coconut milk, stir and bring to the boil. Add the salt and season with some pepper. Leave to simmer for 10-15 minutes.

Whilst this is cooking, move on to cook your cauliflower rice by popping it in a pan with a little extra virgin olive oil on medium heat. Cook for 5 minutes.

Once done, add the spinach to your curry and leave it to wilt for a few seconds/minute and then stir into the rest of the mixture. Serve up with the side of cauliflower rice just before the spinach becomes too limp. Enjoy!

Primal on coconut milk

As it is very dense I don't recommend drinking it like cow's milk. Even though we don't count calories, if you do want it as a stand-alone drink, just go for half a glass. Even this small amount will provide you with 25g of healthy fat, plus a good dose of manganese, copper, phosphorus, magnesium and iron.

TURMERIC CHICKEN

Number of servings: 4   Preparation Time: 8 minutes   Cooking Time: 30 minutes

Turmeric is one of the most powerful natural medicines we can add to our food. It is the richest source of the antioxidant substance known as curcumin.

I personally love to cook lots of dishes with this heaven-sent spice, but at the same time I still take a daily supplement to make sure I am not missing out on the goodness that it packs. After all, the spice is said to reduce the risk of prostate and skin cancer, brain tumours, leukemia, multiple sclerosis and depression. It's a natural painkiller that, for aches and pains in certain parts of the body, is said to be as effective as ibuprofen. Whilst I am a big believer that most research is misleading, as correlation rarely proves causation, I do believe turmeric is part of the reason why in India, where it is consumed by millions, Alzheimer's and Parkinson's is extremely uncommon.

Ingredients

4 chicken breasts (or 8 legs)
8 Primal turmeric capsules (opened)
2 tbsp turmeric (optional)

Black pepper
4 or 5 tbsp coconut oil

Method

We recommend using Primal Turmeric supplements, as they're amongst the very finest on the market. Open the capsules (they are designed for this very purpose) and add to the coconut oil in a bowl.

Add 2 tablespoons of ground black pepper. If you don't have our Primal Turmeric, then take 2 tablespoons of ground turmeric and add that instead. Stir it all together and then coat the chicken.

Cook at gas mark 4 (180 degrees Celsius) for around 30 minutes or until the chicken is thoroughly cooked (when the juices run clear).

Serving suggestion

Serve with Primal chips (page 192), Primal mash (page 190) or roasted vegetables (page 189).

TURKISH BEEF SKEWERS

 Number of servings: 4   Preparation Time: 10 minutes   Cooking Time: 20 minutes

Ingredients

800g lean mince beef
2 red or white onions (finely chopped)
Bell peppers (optional)
1/2 tsp curry powder (optional)

Tabasco (optional)
1/2 tsp cinnamon (ground)
1/2 tsp cayenne (ground)
1 tsp cumin (ground)
Salt and pepper

Method

Start by soaking 8 wooden skewers in water (stops them burning). Place half the meat in a blender and then pour half measures of the other ingredients over the meat. I tend to prepare them in two separate batches, so that I can make some more spicy than others.

Pulse the blender. Whilst you want everything to mix well, it looks nicer if it doesn't just end up as a one big purée (if the lean mince beef is already finely chopped then it's better to use your hands and not the blender).

Next, take the meat out of the blender and shape around the wooden skewers. Then either cook them in the oven at gas mark 4 (180 degrees Celsius) and cook on non-stick baking paper for 20 minutes or alternatively tastes great on a BBQ.

COD FISH FINGERS

🍴 Number of servings: 4 🕐 Preparation Time: 20 minutes 🕐 Cooking Time: 20 minutes

Ingredients

4 cod fillets
Almond flour
2 eggs

1 tsp smoked paprika
Salt and pepper
Coconut oil

Method

With four young children at home who all love supermarket fish fingers, Steve knew he'd have to perfect a Primal-friendly recipe that they'd all enjoy. As they are often prepared with breadcrumbs, yeast, potato starch and other non-Primal ingredients, we were adamant on getting these in. Steve was inspired by a recipe he found in a book called The Paleo Primer, brilliantly written by Keris Marsden and Matt Whitemore.

You will need to cook the cod the day before. Steam it for about 15 minutes and then put it in a blender and pulse (we don't want a purée, so still a bit flaky is good). Take out the fish and if you have one, use a narrow baking tray (I have one I use for my pâté with a hinge to open and close) push it into the bottom, so that its approximately the height of a fish finger. Cover and put in the freezer overnight.

Next day, take it out and with a sharp knife cut into fish finger shapes.

Take two eggs, add the smoked paprika, a pinch of salt and pepper and whisk together. Gently roll the fish into your eggs. Roll the egg-coated fish in the almond flour and shallow fry in coconut oil until all sides look crispy.

Put on a non-stick sheet of baking paper and place in the oven at gas mark 4 (180 degrees Celsius) for approximately 15 minutes.

BEEF STEW

🍴 Number of servings: 4   🕐 Preparation Time: 20 minutes   🕐 Cooking Time: 3-4 hours

Ingredients

600g lean beef (cubes)
300ml beef stock
1/2 cauliflower (separated into florets)
25g almond flour (or 35g for thicker sauce)
3 cloves garlic (finely diced or crushed)

2 tsp beef bouillon paste
200g mushrooms
3 sticks celery (finely sliced)
4 carrots (sliced)
3 tbsp tomato purée
Fresh rosemary
Salt and pepper

Method

Put the beef stock (I like to make the stock a little thicker than normal), tomato purée, beef bouillon, almond flour in a pot and slowly bring to the boil while stirring.

Then put all the vegetables, herbs and beef into a big roasting pot and pour over the stock. If it doesn't cover everything, then you will need to make and add more stock. Add a pinch of salt and pepper and cook until the meat is really tender. Cook on the hob on a low heat (gas mark 3/160 degrees Celcuis) for 3-4 hours.

Primal tip

Even most cheaper cuts of beef will soften up if cooked for 3 to 4 hours.

Salads, Starters and Snacks

PRAWN COCKTAIL

🍴 Number of servings: 4   🕐 Preparation Time: 5 minutes

Ingredients

300g prawns (cooked and peeled)
Primal mayonnaise (see page 184)
Primal tomato ketchup (see page 185)
Tomato purée (optional)
Black pepper (optional)
Tabasco (optional)

8 cherry tomatoes (cut in half)
2 avocados (sliced)
Coriander or parsley
Lettuce (romaine looks best)
Lemon

Method

Mix your homemade mayonnaise with either your homemade tomato ketchup, or if you haven't got any already prepared you can also use tomato purée.

Add in some optional black pepper and tabasco sauce and keep tasting until you achieve your desired flavour.

Toss in the cooked prawns and coat them in the sauce. Serve on a bed of lettuce leaves, with your avocado and cherry tomatoes to the side. Sprinkle on your favourite herbs and squeeze on a little fresh lemon.

PRIMAL THAI SALAD

Number of servings: 4   **Preparation Time: 45 minutes**

Ingredients

2 cups diced kale
4 chicken breasts
5 carrots (shredded)
5 spring onions (sliced diagonally)
1 yellow bell pepper (sliced)
1 red bell pepper (sliced)
1/2 cup coriander (chopped)
4 or 5 romaine lettuce leaves

VARIATIONS (OPTIONAL)
Handful of peanuts or cashews
1 diced red onion to salad

Savoury - add a cup of diced grapefruit
Sweet – add a cup of diced mango or pineapple

SAUCE
Sweet peanut butter
1/2cup natural peanut butter
2 tbsp raw honey
2 cloves of garlic (finely chopped)
3 tbsp lime juice
1 tbsp ginger (finely chopped)
Blend all together, add water or coconut milk if you need to alter texture and toss the salad in into it

Method

Boil the chicken until it is cooked thoroughly. Allow it to cool and then use a rolling pin and bang it until it shreds, or if you prefer try and shred with two forks. Then let it cool.

Above I have listed the ingredients that I always add to my Thai salads. Then a few variations depending on whether my friends eat nuts and two alternative suggestions to make the dish more sweet or savoury. Once you have prepared your salad, toss it all together with the chicken and a sauce (above I have detailed my favourite) and serve on a bed of romaine lettuce leaves.

PORK SALAD

🍴 Number of servings: 4   🕐 Preparation Time: 10 minutes   🕐 Cooking Time: 10 minutes

Ingredients

850g minced pork
Coconut oil
Handful peanuts or cashews
Red or white onion (finely chopped)
Coriander

Spinach
120ml lime juice
120ml fish sauce
Sweet chill sauce

Method

Whenever we have invited friends around for dinner, there is always one dish they always seem to ask if we are cooking and that's our Pork Salad.

Fry the minced pork in the coconut oil. Once cooked, strain and rinse the pork in boiling water. Leave it to cool to room temperature. Finely chop up the onion (uncooked is best) and stir it, along with the lime juice, fish sauce, optional sweet chilli sauce, and minced pork. Put it in a serving bowl and sprinkle some nuts on top (either whole or crushed) and scatter on some chopped coriander. Serve on a bed of spinach leaves.

SCOTCH EGG

🍴 Number of servings: 5   🕐 Preparation Time: 10 minutes   🕐 Cooking Time: 25 minutes

Ingredients

7 eggs
500g lean mince pork
75g almonds (ground) or flaxseeds

Fresh parsley
Salt and pepper

Method

My Dad loves scotch eggs, so the challenge was set to make them Primal!

Hard boil 5 of the eggs. Once cooked, put them in cold water and peel.

Put the minced pork in a blender, along with the fresh parsley, salt and pepper and blend into a purée. Take it out of the blender and separate into 5 equal portions.

Then, flatten out the meat mixture into circles and use your hands to contour it around the eggs. Try not to leave any gaps.

Put the two spare eggs into the blender (no need to wash in-between) and whisk them. Pour the eggs into a bowl and then roll the scotch egg in it.

Roll your meat-covered eggs on a saucer containing the almonds (ground) or flaxseeds (as photographed). Cook for approximately 40 minutes on gas mark 4 (180 degrees Celsius), turning half way through.

CRISPY CHILLI AVOCADO CHIPS WITH PRIMAL TOMATO KETCHUP

Number of servings: 2   Preparation Time: 10-15 minutes   Cooking Time: 35-40 minutes

Recently we decided to get a little adventurous with one of our favourite fruits, avocados, and with the help of the Bennett children, we created a delicious chip recipe after being inspired by a few other recipes. Now, we don't literally mean your crunchy deep fat fried kind of chip. We actually mean a crispy baked avocado chip that's quite frankly, more delicious than it sounds.

We personally think that if you can take an unhealthy recipe and turn it into something much healthier, that's packed with 10x more vitamins and nutrients but still tastes great, then eating healthy can be pretty special.

We decided to get a little creative with the avocado chip coating and believe us, it really does taste like fried crispy breadcrumbs. Pair that with our rich Primal-friendly tomato ketchup sauce and you really will have your taste buds going crazy. Thanks to the flaxmeal flour that's included in the coating of the avocado chip, these little green chips have quite a lot to offer in terms of wellness.

When it comes to making the Primal-friendly tomato ketchup sauce, simply pop all of your ingredients into a food processor and whizz until creamy. This has got to be one of our favourite sauce creations so far! It's rich, boasts a beautiful flavour of deep tomatoes and the oregano compliments the sauce very well. In fact, we have to say we much prefer this tomato ketchup recipe than the original and we're pretty sure you will too!

Ingredients

AVOCADO CHIPS
2 ripe (but still hard) avocados
1 tsp smoked paprika
Pinch of chilli flakes
80g almond flour
20g flaxmeal flour
1 tsp oil (avocado/coconut/extra virgin olive oil)
1 egg
Pinch of salt

PRIMAL TOMATO KETCHUP
1/2 cup tomato purée
1/2 cup tinned tomatoes
1 tbsp raw honey
2 tbsp apple cider vinegar
1/3 fresh onion (diced)
1 tsp oregano
Pinch of salt and pepper

Method

Begin by preheating your oven to gas mark 4 (180 degrees Celsius).

In a bowl mix together the two flours, spices and salt and stir everything together.

In another bowl, crack your egg and whisk. Leave to the side whilst you peel and slice your avocados into thin chip sizes.

One by one, place your avocado chips into your egg bowl and cover completely with the liquid. Remove from the bowl and then cover your chip completely with the flour mix.

Once done, pop your chip onto a baking tray with a little oil and repeat this process until all your avocado chips are covered.

Once done, place your baking tray into the middle of the oven and bake for 20-25 minutes or until golden.

continued...

Remove from the oven and leave to cool. Trust me, these avocado chips are much tastier when enjoyed cool as the avocado hardens back up!

Whilst your chips cool, place all your ketchup ingredients into a food processor and whizz together. Once you have a smooth ketchup paste, pour it into a dipping bowl and enjoy!

HOW TO OPEN AN AVOCADO

Step 1 - Cutting avocado. Cut in half, then twist top clockwise and bottom anti-clockwise.

Step 2 - Removing the huge seed. Very carefully, take sharp knife and chop into seed. Then twist and it should pop out. If it doesn't, scoop it out with a spoon.

Step 3 - Scoop out the fruit using a spoon.

Primal on avocados

While most fruits have numerous health benefits, they are still primarily carbohydrates, so not helpful for us when we are trying to lose a lot of weight, and certainly not good when we consume too many of them. But the superfruit avocado is unique in that it is primarily a fat. There are so many benefits of regularly consuming avocado that, if I had to pick just one food to take on a desert island, it would be a toss up between avocado and coconuts.

Avocados contain an amazing line-up of vitamins and minerals. First of all, they are 77% heart healthy monounsaturated fat, 19% carbohydrates and 4% protein. The majority of fat found in avocado is oleic acid (also known as Omega 9), which also happens to be the super ingredient found in olives. Oleic acids provide numerous health benefits, including helping to reduce inflammation and warding off cancer. They are full of antioxidants that help, among other things, to protect our sight. There are lots of white papers and studies that suggest that having a high intake of potassium helps to reduce blood pressure (a major factor in heart attacks) and avocados have twice that of a large banana!

Avocados also contain large quantities of vitamin B5, B6, C, E, K and folate. They are also a superb source of fibre, and of its huge fibre content, 25% of it is soluble which allows it to feed our friendly gut bacteria.

PRIMAL CHICKEN PATE

🍴 Number of servings: 12　　🕐 Preparation Time: 10 minutes　　🕐 Cooking Time: 20 minutes

It wouldn't be a Primal recipe book if we didn't include my famous chicken liver pâté.

Chicken pâté has always been enjoyable for us both, and thanks to my Primal-friendly version, we all can enjoy it as part of a Primal lifestyle.

Pâté is most well known as being classically French, however, us Brits are no strangers to it – especially when evening parties call.

Just like your typical pâté recipe, my recipe is creamy, smooth and decadent. This version, however, is Primal, low carb and contains all natural ingredients. You'll find that we've used natural and organic chicken livers. We strongly encourage you to go organic too. Shop bought chicken livers are often pumped with added ingredients that are far from good for us.

While chicken is one of the most commonly eaten meats, the liver is often overlooked as an undesirable part of the bird. In fact, chicken liver provides a healthy dose of iron and zinc. This enables your body to use oxygen efficiently, to create new red blood cells and to maintain a healthy immune system. So if you're not a fan of liver, then now is your time to face your fears (seriously, it's not that bad) and get ready to fill your mouths with the natural taste of France!

Ingredients

400g chicken livers (fresh or frozen)
150g unsalted organic butter
2 garlic clove (finely chopped)
3 shallots (finely chopped)
3 sprigs thyme (leaves only)

Pinch of nutmeg (ideally fresh)
2 tsp of fish sauce or 1 spoon of anchovy paste
Sea salt and black pepper (to taste)
Chilli flakes and walnuts (optional)

Method

Trim off any gristle from the chicken livers and roughly dice.

Heat a frying pan and add 30g of butter. Once melted, add chicken livers to the pan and fry on a medium heat for 8 minutes (roughly). Make sure not to burn the livers, they are best when browned on the outside and slightly pink on the inside. Take out of the pan when cooked and place on the side.

Fry the shallots, thyme and garlic till soft. Add the nutmeg, salt and pepper and cook. Pour everything into a food processor (the livers, 120g chopped butter and shallots, thyme and garlic), add the fish sauce and blend.

Check the taste and if needed add more fish sauce or anchovy paste, black pepper as necessary.

Add a small amount of chilli flakes and walnuts at the end and blend for one more short blast (optional).

Once done, spoon the pâté into a sealable jar (we used a mason jar) and pop in the fridge to set. This normally takes a few hours.

The pâté will last for about 5 to 7 days. If you want to store it for longer, melt more butter and put a layer on top.

HOME ROASTED NUTS

🕐 Preparation Time: 2 minutes   🕐 Cooking Time: 30 minutes

On 11th June 2015, The Independent newspaper wrote, "Eating just a handful of nuts a day could lower your risk of a heart attack or of dying from cancer and diabetes". They went on to say, "Epidemiologist Professor Piet van den Brandt, who led the study of more than 120,000 Dutch people between the ages of 55 and 69 at Maastricht University, said the findings were 'remarkable', particularly due to the small amount that needed to be eaten daily to make a difference".

Ingredients

Whatever mixed nuts you like!
Olive oil
Salt and pepper

OPTIONAL
Dark chocolate (more than 75% pure)
Chilli power
Curry powder
Coriander powder
Ground cumin powder

Method

As we mention in our book *The Primal Cure*, it's always best to purchase nuts that are in the baking section of your supermarket, not those near the checkout. You see, most nuts are cooked and coated in all sorts of things that simply aren't at all healthy. What's more, currently in Great Britain there is no value added tax (VAT) on plain nuts that are packaged as an ingredient! So, gram by gram, they are cheaper too!

We've added this home roasted nuts recipe so you can add a little variety to your healthy nut snack

Pre-heat oven to gas mark 3 (160 degrees Celsius). Toss the nuts in the oil so that they are well coated and then evenly sprinkle on your desired amount of salt and pepper and favourite spices (just sprinkle on a pinch at a time). Place them on a sheet of non-stick baking paper (we don't use aluminium as it has been linked with Alzheimer's) on a baking tray and cook for about 30 minutes turning half way through.

If you want to the cover them in chocolate, then melt the chocolate in a separate bowl and dip the nuts in after cooking, then place on non-stick baking paper and put in the fridge to set.

GLAZED NUTS

 Preparation Time: 2 minutes    Cooking Time: 40 minutes

Walnuts, cashews, almonds, pecans, pistachios, Brazil nuts, hazelnuts, macadamias and chestnuts all have numerous health benefits, and can at the same time add real flavour to our Primal lifestyle.

All nuts are rich in protein and healthy oils such as Omega 3. Most of them also contain healthy levels of magnesium, potassium, iron, copper and various vitamin Bs. But with nuts, we do need to demonstrate a little bit of portion control.

Ingredients

250g of whatever mixed nuts you like!
Olive oil
60ml raw honey
1 tbsp ground cinnamon

4 tbsp almond milk (unsweetened, or try making your own)
Salt

Method

This recipe was inspired by one I found in a brilliant book called *Paleo Diet For Brits*. Although you can you use any nuts that you prefer, we think that Glazed Roasted nuts works best with walnuts.

Pre-heat oven to gas mark 3 (160 degrees Celsius). Roast the nuts the same as we do in our Home Roasted Nuts recipe.

Take the honey, cinnamon, almond milk and a pinch of salt and heat in a pan over a medium heat for about 10 minutes. Once it becomes a nice liquid, drop in the nuts and mix. Remove them and separate on non-stick baking paper. When they have completely cooled, store in an air tight glass jar.

Serving suggestion

Mixes well with our coconut crisps
(see page 180).

4 INGREDIENT PRIMAL GRANOLA BARS

Number of servings: 12   **Preparation Time: 5 minutes**   **Cooking Time: 30 minutes**

These bars are simple, sweet, sticky and come with the perfect crunch. To make our Primal bars you'll only need four essential ingredients. However, feel free to add whatever bits and bobs you may fancy. Personally, we wanted a recipe that was very simple and quick to put together but still delivered a sweet and nutty taste.

We've used almonds as the main base for our granola bars as they're one of our favourite nuts thanks to their amazing health benefits. We've also used raw and organic honey – something you may notice that we use quite often when it comes to my Primal bakes.

We'd like to think that these bars are also child-friendly. In fact, Steve's kids love this recipe – just be sure your kids are old enough not to choke on whole nuts (you'll know best). They make for the perfect after school snack!

Ingredients

95g flaked almonds
150g almonds
3 tbsp mixed seeds (we used pumpkin, flax and sunflower seeds)

105 grams raw honey
1 vanilla pod (optional)
1/4 tsp salt (optional)

Method

Begin by preheating your oven to gas mark 3 (160 degrees Celsius).

In a bowl add together all of your ingredients and mix together until everything has combined. This may take a good few minutes for the honey to work it's way around.

Pour the granola mix into a greased baking tray (we use a little coconut oil to grease our tray) and evenly press the granola down so it's packed in tight. Pop into the oven to bake for 25-30 minutes or until golden brown.

Once baked, remove from the oven and leave to cool completely. This is important otherwise you will not be able to cut the granola bars without it crumbling. **DO NOT CUT WARM!**

Once cool, remove, cut your bars pop into an airtight container where they will last for up to a week. These make the perfect snack for those peckish times!

Primal on almonds

They're one of the healthiest nuts you could possibly consume and will provide you with a massive amount of nutrients. One handful of almonds contains roughly 3.5g fibre, 6g protein, 14g fats (all healthy and essential of course) and also contain magnesium, manganese, vitamin E, iron, copper, vitamin B2 and phosphorus.

SALT AND PEPPER KALE CHIPS

 Number of servings: 1 bowl  Preparation Time: 2 minutes  Cooking Time: 25-30 minutes

Ingredients

200g Kale
Coconut oil or olive oil

Salt and pepper

Method

This may sound like an unusual recipe, but believe us, once roasted in the oven, the kale leaves turn into crispy flakes that are almost identical to the texture of traditional crisps. Add a little salt and pepper and you're in for a treat!

Toss the kale in oil. Spread out on a sheet of non stick paper and place in the oven at gas mark 4 (180 degrees Celsius). Keep checking on it after about 10 minutes, it's important that while you do want them crispy, not to let them burn. Cooking time is normally around 15 minutes. Remove from the oven and let them cool.

Thanks to kale being one of the most nutrient-dense foods on the planet, these oven-baked crispy crisps are more than healthy! Did you know that one single cup of kale contains vitamin A, K, C, B6, manganese, calcium, copper, potassium and magnesium? It also contains 3% or more of the DV for vitamin B1, B2, B3, iron and phosphorus.

Steve's kids absolutely love these crisps and they also love getting involved in the making! So next time you've got a spare half an hour, give these kale crisps a go and prove your whole family wrong!

STICKY COCONUT AND NUT GRANOLA BARS

 Number of servings: 16    Preparation Time: 10 minutes    Cooking Time: 45 minutes

Welcome to the chewiest, tastiest and stickiest coconut and nut granola bars you will have ever tried. These bars are Primal-friendly, full of healthy and encouraging fats and contain no CARBS.

These bars contain absolutely no processed ingredients and they simply stick together from the bounding of the desiccated coconut and raw honey.

All in all, we believe that these bars taste just like the kind of granola bars you'd buy in the shops – minus the sugar, unknown ingredients and CARBS! They're sweet, nutty, sticky, and of course, they're deliciously crunchy from the almonds, pecans and crisp golden edges. They're also incredibly easy to make with only 6 main ingredients (the spice is optional).

Ingredients

240g mix of pecans and almonds
130g desiccated coconut
55g coconut oil melted
65g almond butter (or nut butter of choice)

2 tbsp raw honey
1 medium egg beaten
1 tsp spice of choice ginger or cinnamon (we used cinnamon)
1 tsp coconut flour

Method

Begin by preheating your oven to gas mark 4 (180 degrees Celsius).

In a bowl mix together the nuts, desiccated coconut and coconut flour. Set aside.

In another bowl, add the coconut oil, almond butter and honey together. Stir thoroughly together until the mixture is smooth (this may take some time).

Add the beaten egg to the wet ingredients and mix everything together. Next, add the wet ingredients to the dry ingredients and stir until everything is mixed.

Line a square baking tin with parchment paper and pour your granola mixture into the pan and flatten.

Pop your granola bars into the middle of the oven to bake for 30 minutes (or until the edges of your granola bars are golden) and then remove from the oven and flatten the bars down once again with a spatula.

Once done, leave to cool (this is extremely important for the bars to set). Using a sharp knife, cut the granola into 16 bars. You may need to keep flattening the bars as you go to keep their shape. Eat and enjoy!

COFFEE BANANA BREAD

 Number of servings: 10   Preparation Time: 10 minutes    Cooking Time: 45 minutes

---

Primal coffee banana bread that's grain free and packed full of nourishing ingredients. It's moist, light and thanks to the banana and raw honey that's used, it's sweet enough without adding any unnecessary sugar.

The almond butter (raw and all natural) works perfectly. It gives the bread the perfect texture – moist but not too moist – and the nut flavour is hidden thanks to the coffee and banana. Plus, almonds are packed with tons of health benefits including magnesium, copper, vitamin B2, fibre, protein and thanks to their healthy fats, they help reduce hunger levels.

---

2 medium bananas
108g almond butter
3 tbsp raw honey
3 large eggs
90g light coconut flour

2 tbsp coffee granules
1/2 tsp baking powder
1 tsp cinnamon
1 handful crushed pecans for topping (optional)

Method

Begin by preheating your oven to gas mark 4 (180 degrees Celsius) and line a bread tin with foil.

In a bowl, whisk together your eggs for a minute or two. Add your honey and almond butter and mix everything together.

Add the rest of the dry ingredients to the wet and mix everything together (without over mixing - this is important).

Pour your banana mixture into your bread tin and top with broken pecan pieces. Pop in the middle of the oven to bake for 40-45 minutes.

Once cooked, remove from the oven and leave to cool completely. This is important so your slices don't crumble when you cut into them!

Once cool, dig in and enjoy! We always find banana bread is best when slightly toasted - try it! To keep your loaf fresh, simply cover with foil and pop in an airtight container at room temperature. This will keep best for a few days!

COCONUT CRISPS

🍴 Number of servings: 2   🕐 Preparation Time: 10 minutes   🕐 Cooking Time: 20 minutes

While you can in some stores purchase coconut flakes read to go, if you do chose to do this, just try and ensure they are not coated with anything. What I prefer is to buy a fresh coconut, take it outside and break the shell with a hammer. Don't do this on the kitchen worktop, or you are likely to damage something. Once you have broken the shell in several places, simply remove the inside and with a sharp knife slice into thin pieces, about 2mm thick and about 2cm long.

Method

Use a frying pan and cook on high heat, regularly turning the flakes over. You want them to turn slightly brown, but not burnt. No need for any oil, as the coconut flakes have it built in!

Alternatively, you can bake in an oven.

Preheat the oven to gas mark 3 (160 degrees Celsius), pour the coconut flakes onto a sheet of non-stick baking paper baking sheet and cook for about 20 minutes. That's it folks! Store in an airtight container.

- PRIMAL -

Sauces, Sides and more

SUNDRIED TOMATO AND OLIVE BREAD

 Number of servings: 1 loaf   Preparation Time: 10 minutes   Cooking Time: 40 minutes

From the flavours to the texture, this truly is a recipe that will have you thinking that you are indeed, eating a slice of bread. We played around with the recipe a little in order to get the texture right. You see, when you're using ingredients high in healthy fats it can leave you with a slightly oily bake, however, after a few trials, we were left with a beautifully flavoursome bread with the perfect bread texture. Not too oily and not too dense.

Thanks to the olives and sundried tomatoes, you're also left with a stunning display of colours and aroma once you cut into the bread. Although no carbs were used in the making of this bread, it rises and bakes just like a normal loaf of bread would.

Unlike most bread recipes, this Primal sundried tomato and olive bread recipe requires no kneading and no rising time. Simply mix the ingredients together and bake. It really is that simple. Therefore, it makes for the perfect last minute preparations. It's also a great way to encourage friends and family members into living a more Primal lifestyle. In fact, they may not even notice the difference!

Ingredients

225g almond flour

2 tbsp unflavoured whey protein powder

40g mixed seeds (pumpkin seeds, golden linseed and flaxmeal)

Pinch of salt

1/2 tsp baking soda

4 large organic whole eggs

1 egg white

1 tbsp apple cider vinegar

110g mixed olives

70g sundried tomatoes (chopped)

1/2 tsp fresh basil

1/2 tsp fresh oregano

1/2 tsp black pepper

Method

Begin by preheating your oven to gas mark 4 (180 degrees Celsius) and grease an 8" x 8" baking tray. In a bowl mix together the almond flour, protein powder, salt, seeds and baking soda. Add the eggs and apple cider vinegar to the bowl and whisk until everything has combined together. Add the olives, chopped sundried tomatoes and the rest of the seasoning and herbs and carefully mix with a wooden spoon.

Pour your bread mixture into the greased baking tray and pop in the middle of the oven to bake for 40 minutes. Once done and cooked throughout (your oven temperature may differ so check in the middle of the bread), remove your load and leave to cool completely before removing it from the tin. This part is incredibly important to make sure the bread keeps its hold!

Once cool, slice the bread and if possible, toast! This bread is the best toasted as the heat warms the flavours throughout and creates a truly golden crisp outside. Either way, dig in and enjoy!

Primal tip

We recommend that you try toasting your slice of sundried tomato and olive bread before eating. By toasting the bread, it allows the toaster to heat up the flavours inside and provides it with a gorgeous crisp, which in my opinion, really makes this recipe so please do give it a go!

For a plain loaf of bread, simply skip the sundried tomatoes and olives.

PRIMAL MAYO

 Number of servings: 2   Preparation Time: 15 minutes

Ingredients

2 egg yolks
1 1/2 cups olive oil
1/2 freshly squeezed lemon

1/2 tbsp white wine vinegar
3 or 4 pinches sea salt

Method

Make sure the eggs are at room temperature otherwise the mayonnaise might not thicken.

Put the egg yolks, white wine vinegar, Dijon mustard, salt and the lemon juice together in the bottom of a bowl. Let it settle, then pour on top the olive oil.

Then, only using the pulse button on a pulsating hand immersion blender, start at the bottom of the bowl and briefly pulse on and off.

Don't rush, patience is a virtue when it comes to making Primal mayo. Start moving the blender upwards, starting and stopping, until you have a light fluffy mayonnaise.

This is not like supermarket mayo, which will keep in the fridge due to months (thanks to a load of additives) - this is super natural fresh mayo, which will be fine in the fridge for two or three days in a sealed dish.

PRIMAL TOMATO KETCHUP

 Number of servings: 8   Preparation Time: 5 minutes   Cooking Time: 40 minutes

Ingredients

1/2 cup tomato purée
5 fresh tomatoes or 1/2 cup tinned tomatoes
1 tbsp raw honey
2 tbsp apple cider vinegar

1/3 onion (finely chopped)
1 tbsp oregano
Pinch of salt and pepper
1 clove of finely chopped garlic (optional)

Method

Quarter the tomatoes, add a little bit of water and put in a either a saucepan with a lid or a pressure cooker for 5 minutes on gas mark 4 (180 degrees Celsius).

Once cooked, let them cool and then create a purée with a blender. Alternatively use half a can of tinned tomatoes (make sure there is no sugar added).

Add all the other ingredients and cook for about 30 minutes. Take out a teaspoon full, put it on a plate and check there is no water left. If there is cook a little longer.

PRIMAL BATTER

🍴 Number of servings: 1-2   🕐 Preparation Time: 5 minutes   ♨ Cooking Time: 20 minutes

Ingredients

2 eggs
1/2 tsp smoked paprika
Pinch of chilli flakes (optional)

60g almond flour
15g flaxmeal flour
Pinch of salt

Method

In a bowl mix together the two flours, spices and salt and stir everything together.

In another bowl, crack the eggs and whisk.

One by one, place your fish cakes, fish, vegetables or whatever you would like to batter into the egg bowl and cover completely with the liquid.

Remove the food item from the bowl and cover with the flour mix. Once done, pop your food onto a sheet of non-stick baking paper and pop into the oven on a medium heat until crispy. Alternatively, shallow fry in coconut oil or butter.

Primal tip

You can replace both flours with coconut flour. But as we already use our beloved coconut in so many recipes we thought we would provide you with an alternative.

PRIMAL COLESLAW

Number of servings: 8   **Preparation Time: 15 minutes**

Ingredients

Mayonnaise (Homemade see page 184)
1/2 cabbage
6 or 7 carrots (peeled)

Lemon
Salt and pepper
Raw honey (optional)

Method

With either a Julienne Peeler, grater or a spiralizer, cut the cabbage and carrots into thin strips.

Add the homemade mayonnaise, a little salt and black pepper to your acquired taste and then squeeze on the lemon. Toss it all together and if you like it a little sweeter, add a drizzle of honey - job done.

Julienne Peeler

Spiralizer

PRIMAL GUACAMOLE

🍴 Number of servings: 4   🕐 Preparation Time: 10 minutes

Ingredients

4 very soft avocados
2 tomatoes (very finely chopped)

1 lemon or lime
Salt and pepper

Method

Don't throw out those soft avocados. They might no longer be right for our Primal Avocado Chips, but you can certainly make one hell of a guacamole out of them.

Extract the avocado (see page 164) and mash in a bowl. Add in the tomato, squeeze in your lemon or lime and a pinch of salt and pepper to your desired taste. Suggestion of something to serve it with that isn't crisps or nachos!

ROAST VEGETABLES

Number of servings: 6   **Preparation Time: 10 minutes**   **Cooking Time: 30 minutes**

Ingredients

Ghee (or olive oil)
2 onions (quartered)
Red bell peppers (quartered)
Yellow bell pepper (quartered)
Orange bell pepper (quartered)
3 tomatoes (quartered)

2 courgettes (diced diagonally)
4 or 5 carrots (cut into big chunks)
5 or 6 mushrooms (optional)
Garlic (whole) (optional)
Salt
Herbs

Method

Take a very sharp knife and cut the garlic bulb across the top about the quarter of the way down, but don't separate the cloves. With the skin on, completely cover the garlic cover the garlic with ghee or olive oil and put it in the oven as it starts to warm up (it needs a head start on the vegetables).

Cut everything else big and chunky. With the exception of the optional mushrooms, dip each piece in the olive oil and place on a sheet of non-stick baking paper. Next, sprinkle on your favourite herbs and add a little salt. Cook at gas mark 4 (180 degrees Celsius), for about 15 minutes, then turn everything over, add the mushrooms and bake for a further 15 minutes.

We like to serve the garlic on a small plate in the centre of the table and let everyone help themselves. If properly cooked, the outer skin should just fall off.

Tip: To get the kids to eat more vegetables, try serving them kebab style on a skewer.

PRIMAL MASH

Number of servings: 4   Preparation Time: 3 minutes   Cooking Time: 10 minutes

BUTTERNUT SQUASH

Ingredients

2 tbsp greek yogurt
2 tbsp herbs (sage, theme, rosemary etc)
Salt and pepper

Method

Slice into quarters or cut in half and steam the butternut squash for around 7 to 10 minutes.

Next scoop out and discard the seeds and add two tablespoons of natural Greek yogurt, a pinch of salt and pepper and then either mash or blend into a purée.

The reason I add the yogurt, is not only is it super healthy, it gives a really nice creamy texture to the mash.

CAULIFLOWER MASH

2 tbsp herbs (sage, theme, rosemary etc)
1 or 2 cloves garlic (minced)
Salt and pepper
Olive oil

Steam the cauliflower for around 7 to 10 minutes until it's cooked but not too soft. Drain and put in a bowl.

Fry the garlic in 3 tbsp of olive oil and pour on top of the cooked cauliflower. Sprinkle on your herbs, a pinch of salt and pepper, and either mash or blend into a purée.

Alternatively, you can boil butternut squash. Remove the central softened flesh and then follow the same process as with cauliflower.

PRIMAL RICE

🍴 Number of servings: 4   🕐 Preparation Time: 5 minutes   🕐 Cooking Time: 10 minutes

Ingredients

2 cauliflowers (grated)
1 tbsp olive oil
Salt and pepper

1 garlic clove (minced) (optional)
Onion (finely chopped) (optional)
1 cup vegetable stock

Method

Use a large-holed cheese grater to grate the cauliflower (or carefully pulse it in a food processor).

Fry the garlic and onion in 1 tbsp of olive oil for about 5 minutes and then add the cauliflower and vegetable stock (this is optional but it gives a nice soft texture) and cook gently for a further 5 minutes or so. Sprinkle on the salt and pepper and you are done! Goes so well with Thai or Indian curry.

Primal tip

Be sure to be gentle while stirring, otherwise you end up with cauliflower mash.
Whilst mash still tastes great, it doesn't always look right with curries or chillies.

PRIMAL CHIPS

🍴 Number of servings: 1   🕐 Preparation Time: 15 minutes   🕐 Cooking Time: 40 minutes

Ingredients

Carrots or parsnips
Ghee (or goose fat or coconut oil)
Salt

Dried thyme (optional)
Black pepper (optional)
Chilli powder (optional)

Method

The key to getting your kids to love these is to make them look like real chips. Practice with a sharp knife cutting your vegetables to the same shape as the chips your kids like. Most kids have been brainwashed by the big fast food giants to expect thing and long chips (or fries).

If the oil has set, melt it, but don't make it too hot to handle!

Pre-heat the oven to gas mark 4 (180 degrees Celsius). Dip the chips into a bowl of oil and then if you want to sprinkle on salt and herbs, go for it.

Put them on a sheet of non-stick baking paper, making sure to spread them out. Half way through cooking, be sure to turn them over.

For adults, you can always spice them up with black pepper and chilli powder.

COURGETTE SPAGHETTI (COURGETTI)

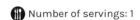 Number of servings: 1    Preparation Time: 10 minutes    Cooking Time: 10 minutes

Ingredients

1 large courgette

Method

If you're not a fan of courgettes, you can also make vegetable spaghetti out of butternut squash or carrots. If you have a Julienne Peeler or a spiralizer then making your own vegetable spaghetti is really easy. If you don't, most large supermarkets are now selling the vegetables in packs already cut into perfectly looking spaghetti, just make sure no other ingredients have been added.

You simply spiralize or julienne cut your courgette, skin and all (it's the best part of the courgette, after all). A picture would be helpful here.

Now, while some people sauté them, we prefer to simply steam them or even put them in a microwave for a minute or two. Be careful to not overcook or you end up with a soggy mess. But if cooked right, they taste great and you can always sprinkle on your favourite herbs. If for some reason they don't float your boat, be sure to try Shirataki noodles (see them on page 148), but never revert back to your old pasta, as its completely void of nutrients and once digested turns into sugar.

COCOA AND CACAO

Cacao powder is made by cold-pressing unroasted cocoa beans. While the process retains many of the beneficial nutrients, it does lose most of its gloriously health fat (cacao butter).

We recommend keeping both a jar of raw unroasted cacao (pronounced 'cacow') powder and cocoa butter in your Primal pantry and, whenever you need to make some sweet desserts for friends, you will be able to fool them that your chocolate-looking dish is no different to the regular sugar-infused milk chocolate they consume. But of course there is a difference, a huge difference.

The rawest of all chocolates, cacao contains more than 250 different nutritional ingredients, making it possibly the best source of antioxidants from plants on the planet! Rich in polyphenols, it even has more than a dozen times more antioxidants than the superfruit blueberries. No wonder the Aztecs used cocoa beans as a currency.

In his book, Tales from the Medicine Trail, author Chris Kilham says, "If cocoa were a pharmaceutical drug, it would be hailed the greatest medicine of all time, and its discoverer would reap the Nobel Prize in Medicine".

Puddings and Desserts

PEANUT BUTTER CHOCOLATE CHIP COOKIES

🍴 Bakes: 14 cookies   🕐 Preparation Time: 5 minutes   🕐 Cooking Time: 10 minutes

Flourless, grain free, natural ingredients and high in healthy fats, these Primal Peanut Butter Chocolate Chips Cookies make for the perfect Primal dessert or snack. With absolutely no flour of any kind required, you can whip these mouth-watering cookies up in just under 15 minutes with the simplest ingredients.

You may be wondering how on earth these chocolate chip cookies may be Primal-friendly but, by using natural and organic peanut butter along with 85% dark chocolate, these cookies are 100% Primal-friendly. And yes, that's including the chocolate too! You will also find that we have added our Primal maca root extract. This provides the cookies with added health benefits, as well as providing the cookies with a delicious hint of caramel.

Unlike the traditional sugary, toxic fat filled and high carbohydrate cookie, these Primal cookies are a little less sweet. However, please feel free to add a little more coconut sugar (or stevia) if a sweet treat is what you're truly after!

Ingredients

255g natural peanut butter
55g raw honey
1 tbsp coconut sugar
1/2 tsp baking soda
Pinch of salt

The powder from 1 *Primal Cure* maca root extract Capsule (simply break the capsule in half to access the powder)
1 free range egg
60g 85% dark chocolate (cut into chunks)

Method

Begin by preheating your oven to gas mark 4 (180 degrees Celsius) and line a baking tray with parchment paper.

In a mixing bowl add all of your ingredients together (except the dark chocolate) and mix on medium speed until you get a dough texture.

Once you have the right texture, add the chocolate chunks and mix again.

Using a tablespoon, add small cookie dough balls (roughly 14) to a baking tray. Leave space for your cookies to expand. Continue until all the dough has been used and then lightly flatten each ball.

Pop your tray into the middle of the oven to bake for 10 minutes. You'll want a slight golden brown appearance for the perfect cookie - crunchy on the outside, soft in the middle.

Once cooked, remove from the oven and leave to cool completely. This is an extremely important step to allow the cookies to harden up.

Once cooled, dig in! To store your Primal peanut butter chocolate chip cookies, pop them in an airtight container and consume within 5 days. If you're saving these for a later date, then you can store the cookies in the freezer and defrost a few hours before consuming.

Chocolate may prevent cancer

As if powerful antioxidants weren't enough, natural dark chocolate is also believed to help prevent cancer. Studies in cancer prevention are still emerging but so far the properties of cocoa found in dark chocolate suggests that the combination of antioxidants (particularly flavonoids), along with how chocolate can make us feel (yes it really does affect our endorphins) has the possibility to fight off cancer.

ALMOND AND COCONUT DARK CHOCOLATE CHERRY TART

 Number of servings: 6-8   Preparation Time: 15 minutes   Cooking Time: 10-12 minutes

King size almond and coconut soft crust pastry tarts, filled with deep and rich organic chocolate, nestled with hints of fresh cherry. The tarts of all tarts if you will. In my opinion, this really does have to be the best Primal tart I've made (and tasted!) to date. The combination of the sweet cherries works beautifully well against the rich dark chocolate and the soft pastry, which crumbles in your mouth with the first bite, complements the richness and brings a softer flavour to the tarts.

We had a lot of fun with this recipe actually. Although it looks quite complicated to make, it really can be made in less than 25 minutes (including baking time) and includes only 8 ingredients - all organic and as natural as possible.

When eaten in moderation, this makes the perfect Primal dessert and it'd be rude not to share with your family and friends! Do not be fooled, whilst 3 thick tarts are photographed, please feel free to thin out the tart pastry and make a few more tarts. I simply went for three chunky mouth-watering tarts for my friends and family to share between them. One individual tart can easily be shared between two (or three) people - if you're not feeling too greedy. If you're after some extra indulgence and gooey goodness, then try microwaving the tarts for just a few seconds before tucking in. It completely changes the texture of the tarts and instantly doubles the indulgence!

Ingredients

95g coconut flour
25g almond flour
25g flaked almonds and 2 tbsp for topping
55g and 1tsp raw honey
1/4 tsp salt

55g solid coconut oil (room temperature - butter like texture)
2 tbsp full fat coconut milk
200g 85%+ dark chocolate
1/2 cup organic fresh cherries (diced, and extra for topping)

Method

Begin by pre-heating your oven to gas mark 4 (180 degrees Celsius) and grease 3 mini tart tins (or one 9" tart tin) with coconut oil.

In a mixer add together the coconut flour, almond flour and flaked almonds and stir. Add the honey, solid coconut oil and salt and mix everything together until you have a solid ball of dough. You also want to make sure that you have no lumps of coconut oil.

If using 3 mini tart tins, then divide your dough into 3 even balls, pop them into the tins and spread out and up the sides. Do this for all 3 tins. If you're using a 9" tart tin then simply do the same but for one tin.

Place in the middle of the oven and bake for 10-12 minutes or until golden brown. Once done, remove from the oven and leave to cool.

Method

Heat a pan with boiling water and place a heat proof bowl on top. Add the chocolate and simmer until all the chocolate has melted. Once done, add 1-2 tbsp of coconut milk to your diced cherries. Stir until everything is mixed together and fill your tarts with the chocolate. The chocolate will start to harden once you add the milk but this will help you set the chocolate in a swirl patter. Once done, pop them in the fridge until the chocolate cools and then remove and top with extra cherries.

If you prefer hard tarts then keep these in an airtight container in the fridge. However, if you'd like these tarts to be a little softer (the best way to have them in my opinion) then keep them in an airtight container at room temperature. Just make sure it's not too hot otherwise the chocolate will melt!

Primal on cherries

They offer a healthy dose of fibre, antioxidants, and vitamins and minerals including vitamin A, folic acid and calcium. Cherries are also known for reducing inflammation in the body as they protect our blood cells from damage caused by oxidants and free radicals.

HEALTHY RASPBERRY PROTEIN BROWNIE BARS

 Number of servings: 12   Preparation Time: 10 minutes   Cooking Time: 23 minutes

We've been trialling a protein brownie bar recipe for quite some time now and finally, we've come up with a delicious – chocolate filled – raspberry brownie bar that's healthy, 100% Primal-friendly, contains no processed CARBS, and is gluten, dairy and sugar-free! In fact, the main ingredient is black beans!

Whilst these beans still contain CARBS, they are indeed a natural and Primal-friendly carb that's full of nutrients, including protein and fibre.

We designed this recipe to be something you can whip up at the beginning of the week to snack on throughout. Despite this being a rather chocolatey recipe, we've not actually used any raw chocolate. Instead, we've used organic WHEY protein powder and cacao powder to create the creamy chocolate flavour.

We won't lie and say this brownie recipe tastes exactly like a gooey, sugar-filled brownie, but it's close enough! Our healthy raspberry protein brownie bars are cakey on the outside and fudgy and sweet on the inside.

Ingredients

50g WHEY protein powder unflavoured or vanilla
245g black beans drained
50g raw honey
50g coconut oil
20g cacao powder

1 tsp baking powder
1 tsp coconut sugar
40g whole raspberries
40g broken raspberries
1 vanilla pod (if not using vanilla protein powder)

Method

Begin by preheating your oven to gas mark 4 (180 degrees Celsius). In a food processor add the drained black beans, honey and vanilla pod and whizz together. Once smooth, add the WHEY, coconut oil, baking powder and coconut sugar. Whizz again until smooth.

Add the cacao powder to the mixture and finally, blend everything together again.

Add the 40g of the whole raspberries to the mixture and stir with a spoon. Be careful not to over stir or you'll break the raspberries.

Pour the brownie mixture into an 8x8 tin and then top with the other 40g of broken raspberries. Pop in the oven to bake for 20-23 minutes. Cook for less if you prefer a gooey brownie.

Once done, remove from the oven and leave to cool before cutting. These are best kept in an airtight container and in the fridge for a few days. If you're using fresh raspberries then remember they go off quickly!

SINGLE SERVE LOW CARB LEMON DRIZZLE CAKE

Number of servings: 1 | **Preparation Time: 5 minutes** | **Cooking Time: 15 minutes**

Our take on the classic lemon drizzle cake is low in CARBS, contains no refined sugar or grains and is 100% Primal-friendly. On top of that, it's refreshingly sweet, moist and fluffy. If you're also familiar with the texture that coconut flour creates, then you'll know that it can create a super fluffy texture and can often look undercooked at times. Don't fret though; it is cooked – just incredibly light and fluffy.

The lemon drizzle is something we're particularly fond of the most when it comes to this recipe. We've managed to create a drizzle by using a vanilla whey protein powder (any protein powder will do), lemon juice and just enough milk and believe us, it tastes delicious!

Ingredients

1 tbsp almond flour
1 1/2 tbsp coconut flour (reduced fat)
3 tbsp raw honey
1 tbsp lemon peel
1 large egg
1/2 tsp baking powder
1 tbsp lemon juice

DRIZZLE
2 tbsp whey protein
1 tsp lemon juice
1 vanilla pod
Enough water to make into a paste

Method

Begin by preheating your oven to gas mark 4 (180 degrees Celsius).

In a bowl mix together your flours, lemon peel and baking powder until combined. In another bowl, whisk together your egg, lemon juice and raw honey.

Add the dry ingredients to the wet and stir until everything has mixed together.
Pour your mixture into a small ramekin dish and pop in the middle of the oven to bake for 15 minutes.

Remove from the oven when you can insert a knife into the middle and it comes out clean.

To make the lemon drizzle simply add enough water to the whey protein powder, vanilla and lemon juice until you reach a drizzle consistency. You may need to stir a lot for this.

Once your cake is cool, pour on the lemon drizzle, add a little lemon peel and tuck in!

Cooking caution

Don't make the mistake we did when it came to pouring the drizzle on top of the lemon when still warm. If you do, then you'll end up with a melted, drooping, disappointing drizzle!

LOW CARB RHUBARB AND STRAWBERRY CRUMBLE SKILLET

Number of servings: 4 • Preparation Time: 10 minutes • Cooking Time: 35 minutes

Rhubarb and strawberry crumble will always be a recipe that pulls at our dessert heartstrings. While we may not be huge dessert fans, we will always hold a special place for a warm crumble in our stomachs - especially now that we've managed to turn the classic CARB heavy crumble into a low carb, Primal-friendly recipe!

Not only is our rhubarb and strawberry crumble skillet extremely healthy, but it's also a true dessert pleaser thanks to its sweet and refreshing flavourings. Our favourite part is the crisp golden crumble that sits on top of the sweet and warm fruits. The crumble itself is made from almond flour, a little raw honey, coconut oil and almond pieces. Altogether it creates a delicious low carb crumble that tastes as good as the real thing.

Ingredients

140g rhubarb (diced)
175g strawberries (diced)
2 tbsp raw honey
1 tbsp coconut sugar
1/4 tsp cinnamon
1 tsp lemon juice
Pinch of salt
1 lemon peel

CRUMBLE TOPPING
105g almond flour
30g coconut flour
2 tbsp raw honey
2 tbsp solid coconut oil
1 tsp cinnamon
60g chopped almonds

Method

Begin by preheating your oven to gas mark 4 (180 degrees Celsius). In a bowl mix together the fruit, honey, coconut sugar, lemon juice and peel, salt and cinnamon.

In a separate bowl, mix together the crumble topping using your fingers to work your way through the solid coconut oil. Rub it until you can no longer feel balls of coconut oil.

Once done, pour the fruit mix into a skillet and layer evenly. Top with your crumble and place the skillet into the middle of the oven to bake for 35 minutes (or until golden). We like our crumble bubbling and very golden brown.

Once baked, remove from the oven and leave to cool for a minute or two. Grab some forks and dig in!

Primal on rhubarb

Rich in fibre, rhubarb has been used for centuries in Chinese medicine to help soothe stomach ailments, disorders and constipation. It's also known to be used for relieving fevers and swelling in the body. With each serving of rhubarb you'll get 45% of the recommended daily amount of vitamin K and you'll also be supporting healthy bone growth.

CARAMELISED STRAWBERRY AND COCONUT PRIMAL ICE CREAM

 Number of servings: 1 tub   Preparation Time: 15 minutes   ❄ Freezing Time: 1 - 2 hours

You'll find that there are tons of Paleo ice cream recipes out there that consist of just fruit and coconut milk, however, our recipe includes the most Primal-friendly ingredients and, by using a secret ingredient, we've managed to make it as creamy and light as possible. On top of that, we've decided to upgrade your classic strawberry ice cream with a little caramel flavour for a truly indulgent, yet perfectly healthy, sweet and mouth-watering treat.

The top secret ingredient? Chia seeds. You'll be amazed at how good these little seeds are for creating a thick and jelly-like texture. Despite their small size, chia seeds are packed full of important nutrients.

Ingredients

2 punnets of fresh strawberries
2 x 400g cans of full-fat coconut milk
1 tbsp raw honey
1 tsp organic coconut oil

1/4 cup chia seeds
1/2 cup extra fresh strawberries (for chunks)
1 tsp cinnamon

Method

Warm a pan with 1 teaspoon of coconut oil and add 2 punnets of strawberries. Drizzle a tablespoon of honey over the strawberries, add the cinnamon and brown the strawberries on medium heat for 5 minutes.

Once caramelised, remove and place the strawberries in a food processor. Add the coconut milk and chia seeds and blitz until smooth.

On the side, chop 1/2 cup of extra fresh strawberries into chunks and pop them into the food processor and mix by hand.

Once done, pour your ice cream mix into a bread loaf tin/tub and place in the freezer to set for 1 - 2 hours.

When ready, remove from the freezer and leave to defrost until you have a creamy soft serve texture.

Primal on chia seeds

They're an excellent source of Omega-3 fatty acids, fibre, iron and calcium and are rich in antioxidants. Well known benefits of chia seeds, when included in our daily diet, including the reduced risk of obesity, heart disease, diabetes, increased energy and the promotion of a healthy complexion (thanks to those fatty acids).

PRIMAL HAZELNUT CHOCOLATE TRUFFLES

🍴 Number of servings: 24 truffles 🕐 Preparation Time: 10 minutes  🕐 Cooking Time: 10 minutes

These Primal hazelnut chocolate truffles are going to blow your mind. Simple. It's not every day you come across a chocolate truffle that's free from refined sugar and packed full of health benefiting ingredients. In fact, this recipe doesn't contain a single ingredient that isn't Primal-friendly – from the truffle to the outside dark chocolate coating.

They're creamy, rich, moreish and most importantly, healthy. The best bit? The crunch you receive from the nutty and rich dark chocolate shell on the outside just before you reach the creamy hazelnut centre - simply delicious!

Ok, now it's time to let you in on a little secret. This recipe includes one key ingredient and it's a vegetable. Can you have a guess as to what it is? Chickpeas. Yes, you heard right and no, we're not pulling your leg! This recipe contains 1 whole tin of chickpeas and it makes up for the creamy chocolate truffle centre.

No, we're still not pulling your leg. You see, the addition of the cacao powder removes any flavouring of the chickpeas and instead, you're left with a chocolatey, creamy truffle centre.

Ingredients

1 tin chickpeas
100g hazelnut butter
3 tbsp cacao powder
3 tbsp raw honey
1 pinch salt

1 vanilla pod
100g melted 85% dark chocolate (or more)
50g chopped hazelnuts (for coating)

Method

Begin by draining your chickpeas and rinsing them. Add the chickpeas, hazelnut butter, cacao powder, honey, vanilla pod and salt to a food processor and blend for a few minutes until you have a creamy texture.

Once done, roll the truffle mixture into small balls and lay them on a tray with parchment paper.

Using a fork, dip each truffle into your melted bowl of dark chocolate and cover them fully with chocolate. Once done, sprinkle a few chopped hazelnuts onto the tray where your truffle will sit back down. Place the chocolate covered truffle back down onto the tray and finish with sprinkling the top with more hazelnuts. Now you should have a full covered truffle with chocolate and hazelnuts. Repeat this process until all truffles are covered.

Once done, pop the tray into a freezer to allow the chocolate to set for 5-10 minutes. Remove from the freezer and dig in!

These truffles will keep best in an airtight container in the fridge for a few days.

HEALTHY CHOCOLATE
YOGHURT EASTER EGGS

 Number of servings: 12   Preparation Time: 5 minutes Cooking Time: 1 hour

Nowadays, the words chocolate and healthy are rarely seen in the same sentence together. If they are, it's often thanks to very clever labelling that claims 'reduced sugar' or 'fat-free' is redeemed as 'healthy', when in fact, it's anything but healthy.

We've used one of our favourite baking ingredients in this recipe, raw cacao powder, and it really is simple to make. All you need are three ingredients and two silicone Easter Egg moulds. Give yourself five minutes to mix the ingredients together in a bowl, an hour to freeze your chocolate yoghurt Easter eggs and bam, you have yourself a perfectly healthy chocolate treat.

Ingredients

500g greek yoghurt organic
2 tbsp cacao powder

1 vanilla pod

Method

In a bowl, mix together all of your ingredients until everything is combined and lump free.

Grab your two silicone egg moulds and dollop a tbsp of mixture into each Easter egg mould. Make sure each mould is level and not overflowing. Repeat this for each mould.

Once done, pop your moulds in the freezer and freeze for an hour (or more if you have time).

Remove them from the freezer, pop the eggs out and enjoy! Steve's kids like to wait until the eggs melt a little for the ultimate creamy treat. Think of it as a mini Easter egg popsicle!

Example

An easter egg mould looks similar to this. Made out of bendy plastic to be able to pop the moulds out when set.

Dairy free option

Simply replace the yoghurt for a dairy free one! In fact, coconut yoghurt would make a lovely combination with the cacao. Go on, give these a go and surprise the children with a healthy treat that's still packed with the creamy taste of chocolate.

Primal post work out treat

Because of their high protein content (from the yoghurt), these would also make for a great post workout treat. Or, if you want to increase the protein value, then simply replace the cacao powder with a scoop of your favourite chocolate protein powder.

CRUNCHY WALNUT TOPPED CARROT CAKE MUFFINS

 Number of servings: 12   Preparation Time: 10 minutes   Cooking Time: 25 minutes

These aren't just your ordinary carrot cake muffins. Oh no, these are our crunchy walnut topped carrot cake muffins and are completely Primal-friendly. Grain free, low CARB and sugar-free has never tasted so good!

They're incredibly moist thanks to them being grain free and they still boast all the flavours of a classic carrot cake. Spice and all things nice. We also love the addition of the crunchy walnut top.

Ingredients

220g almond flour
80g raw honey
115g shredded carrot
136g apple sauce homemade
47g raisins
90g walnut pieces half (for topping)
3 medium eggs
1 tsp lemon peel

1 1/2 tsp cinnamon
1/4 tsp nutmeg
1/4 tsp ginger
2 cloves
1 vanilla pod
1 tsp baking soda
1/2 tsp baking powder

Method

Begin by preheating your oven to gas mark 4 (180 degrees Celsius). In a bowl whisk together your eggs and then add the honey, lemon peel and apple sauce. Stir until everything is combined.

In another bowl add together your dry ingredients (minus the raisins, walnuts and carrots) and stir. Now add the carrots, raisins and half of the walnuts to the mixture and stir until everything is combined.

Add the dry to the wet ingredients and fold everything together.

Using an ice-cream scoop, spoon even mixtures of your carrot cake batter into muffin/cupcake holders and repeat until you have used up all of your mixture.

Finish by topping them with further broken walnut pieces (the smaller the better).

Pop them in the oven to bake for 20-25 minutes or until a knife comes out clean when inserted into the middle of them.

Leave to cool and then dig in!

Kid friendly

Because these muffins contain nothing but healthy and Primal-friendly ingredients, these carrot cake muffins can be enjoyed as a breakfast alternative for the kids or, as a snack to cure of those grumbling tummies in the afternoon.

Primal on apple sauce

While the homemade apple sauce may sound a little demanding at first, believe us, it couldn't be any easier. Simply grab a cooking apple, peel it, cut it into chunks, then pop it in a pan with a little water and a tablespoon of coconut sugar (optional) and bring to the boil. Once done, simply simmer until the chunks of apple go soft and are easy enough to mash into a purée. By creating our own apple sauce we know exactly what's going into the ingredients. No refined sugar, no CARBS and definitely no unhealthy ingredients we can't pronounce.

PRIMAL LOW CARB HOT CROSS BUNS

 Number of servings: 8   Preparation Time: 10 minutes   Cooking Time: 20 minutes

We'll admit, taking the classic hot cross bun recipe and turning it into a Primal-friendly recipe wasn't the easiest of bakes. However, after a little baking science and turning the classic recipe into a grain free one, we were able to whip up these incredibly flavoursome and healthy hot cross buns, which we're sure you're going to love.

Not only do these Primal buns still manage to capture the exact spices of the traditional hot cross bun but, they're incredibly moist, soft and sweet. We decided to stick to raisins for this recipe as the traditional mixed fruit can sometimes become a little overpowering, not to mention high in sugar and CARBS too.

We'd recommend eating these fresh out of the oven or toast/grill them a little to get that added crisp. They're incredibly moist thanks to the good fat's from the almond flour so we're not sure butter is even needed!

Ingredients

300g almond flour
25g coconut oil (solid state)
45g raisins
Pinch of salt
2 tbsp raw honey
1 large orange (the zest of it)
1 vanilla pod
2 large whisked eggs
1 tbsp cinnamon

1/4 tsp nutmeg
1/4 tsp ginger
1 crushed clove

FOR THE CROSSES AND GLAZE
2 tbsp coconut flour
Enough water to form a paste to pipe
1 tbsp raw honey

Method

Begin by preheating your oven to gas mark 4 (180 degrees Celsius).

In a bowl, mix together your dry ingredients (including the raisins) and set aside.

In a microwavable bowl, heat your coconut oil until it melts. Once it's melted leave it to cool down and then add your honey and whisked eggs. Stir until everything is combined.

Grate your orange and add the zest to your dry ingredients and mix everything together. Once done, add the wet ingredients to your dry ingredients and stir until everything is combined and you have a stiff dough.

Line a baking tray with parchment paper and using your hands, create a small round ball with the dough and place on the tray. Repeat this until you've used up all of your dough. You should have about eight hot cross buns and they should all be roughly even in size.

Using the palm of your hand, slightly flatten the balls and using half of your honey, glaze each ball.

Once done, pop them in the oven to bake for 20-25 minutes or until golden.

Remove your hot cross buns from the oven and once again, coat them with the remaining honey and leave to cool.

Whilst they are cooling, make your cross mixture by simply adding enough water to your coconut flour until a paste forms. Pop this in a small piping bag and pipe crosses onto your buns.

Once done, remove your buns from the baking tray, serve and enjoy!

LEMON, CHIA AND COCONUT ENERGY BALLS

 Number of servings: 20   Preparation Time: 5-10 minutes   Cooking Time: 30 minutes

These lemon, chia and coconut energy balls are packed full of healthy and essential fats which means, like all Primal foods, they'll leave us feeling fuller for longer.

This recipe includes a good amount of healthy fats and absolutely no CARBS at all! Instead, they are full of nourishing ingredients from coconuts to chia seeds. The best bit about this recipe? It creates 20 servings! That's an energy ball a day for 20 days (if you don't end up sharing, of course!)

For this recipe, we've included a few of our favourite baking ingredients that make for a primal recipe. We've got coconuts cashews, lemon, chia seeds and raw honey. That's it - no extra sugar. This recipe calls for wholesome, unprocessed ingredients that contain nothing but health benefits for our bodies.

Gym goers might find that the texture of our energy balls are somewhat different from traditional energy balls. However, the reason being is because most energy balls are made with oats, CARBS or dates to help them stick together. Our Primal energy balls, however, are held together by pulsed cashews, coconut flour, coconut and raw honey. Therefore you'll find that the texture of these balls are a lot smoother and less sticky, which if we're honest, we much prefer!

Ingredients

190g whole cashews salted
20g coconut flour
60g desiccated coconut (30g for the balls- 30g for coating)

4 large lemons (you'll be using the juice)
1 1/2 tbsp raw honey
1 tbsp coconut milk
2 tbsp chia seeds

Method

Pop the cashews in a food processor and blitz until fine.

Add the rest of the ingredients (only 30g of desiccated coconut) to the food processor and again, blitz everything together until all ingredients form together.

Roll your dough out onto a surface and then create 20 small balls (about an inch) by rolling the dough out between your hands and then over the remaining desiccated coconut to coat them with.

Place your balls onto a tray once done and then pop them in the freezer for about 15 minutes to harden a little.

After 15 minutes, remove them from the freezer and then pop them in an airtight container and keep them in the fridge ready for snacking!

Primal on chia seeds

Chia seeds are an exceptional superfood that are often overlooked, but actually, they contain many benefits and are highly valued for their medicinal properties. They're also rich in fibre, omega-3 fats, vitamins, minerals and protein. They improve our digestive system, help protect our skin from ageing, inflammation and free radical damage and help to promote heart health.

PRIMAL CARROT LOAF

 Number of servings: 8   Preparation Time: 15 minutes   Cooking Time: 50 minutes

This loaf is everything a carrot loaf should be (just a lot healthier). It's moist, moreish and dense with the amazing flavours that a carrot cake has to offer. From cinnamon, ginger, mixed spice and more, it's a surprisingly healthy loaf!

To make this a Primal-friendly recipe we've kept it grain free with the use of coconut and almond flour. We're also made it refined sugar free by using a little raw organic honey. To bring the loaf together we've used coconut oil, eggs and pumpkin purée. All of these ingredients are Primal-friendly however, when it comes to the honey (which our ancestors did indeed have), we've limited its quantity as much as possible. Although it's a Primal ingredient, we are aware just how addictive and unhealthy sugar can be. Yes, honey is still sugar!

Ingredients

2 cups almond flour
2 tbsp coconut flour
3 large eggs
2 tbsp coconut oil
1/3 cup pumpkin purée homemade
(not canned)
1/3 cup grated carrots

1 tsp cinnamon
1/2 tsp ginger
1/2 tsp mixed spice
1 tsp vanilla extract
1 tsp baking soda
1/2 cup walnuts
3 tbsp raw honey

Method

Begin by pre heating your oven to gas mark 4 (180 degrees Celsius) and lining a bread tin with parchment paper.

In a bowl whisk together your eggs, honey, coconut oil and vanilla extract. Once your wet ingredients are mixed together add your pumpkin purée and whisk again.

In a separate bowl, add together your dry ingredients and mix everything together.

Slowly, add your dry ingredients to your wet ingredients, making sure to stir as you do.

Once your wet and dry ingredients are mixed together, turn the whisk on and finish off the mixing Mix in your walnuts and then pour the mixture into your bread tin.

Before popping your loaf into the oven, sprinkle the top of your carrot loaf mixture with cinnamon and a few more crushed walnuts.

Place your loaf into the middle of the oven to bake for 50 minutes. Once cooked, remove from the oven and leave to cool thoroughly before slicing. Enjoy!

Portion control

Whilst this recipe may not score a 10/10 on our Primal recipe rater (due to the honey content), it's probably one of the healthiest and most primal sweet recipes that you could bake for the entire family. Just remember, moderation and portion control is important! It's easy to get carried away with sweet treats like these... even homemade ones! Our tip for moderation would be to enjoy a slice and then freeze the rest for later.

STICKY CARAMEL APPLES

🍴 Number of servings: 6   🕐 Preparation Time: 20 minutes   🕐 Coating Time: 5 minutes

I've taken the classic sticky toffee apple recipe and simply turned it into a Primal-friendly recipe that contains no refined sugar and only natural carbohydrates. So, how exactly do we make a healthy Primal-friendly caramel sauce? By using Mother Nature's gift of dates! Thanks to the natural sweetness of the dates, you really don't need to add much else to the sauce as the natural sweetener of the dates should be enough. If not, then please feel free to a tablespoon of raw organic honey.

To give the dates a true caramel taste, I've added 2 capsules of our Primal Maca Root. If you're not aware, then the powder of maca has a slight nutty/caramel taste. Therefore, it's wonderful to include in Primal bakes when you're looking to add extra goodness and health benefits to your creations. Just like dates, maca powder has many health benefits including balancing hormones, improving menstrual problems and fertility, increasing mood, fighting depression, boosting libido levels and increasing bone health. However, it's mostly known for its sexual/hormone health benefits.

Ingredients

300g pitted dates
1/2 cup leftover date water
2 *Primal Cure* Maca Root capsules
(simply twist and break to access
the powder)

1 tbsp raw honey (optional)
Pinch salt (optional)
6 apples of choice
6 tbsp desiccated coconut
6 lollipop sticks

Method

In a jug, add your pitted dates and cover them with boiling water. Leave them to soak for 15 minutes. Whilst the dates soak, pierce your apples through the core with skewers/lollipop sticks.

Once soaked, drain the liquid into a separate jug and keep 1/2 cups worth of the soaked date water.

In a food processor add the dates, 1/2 cup date liquid, maca root, vanilla and pinch of salt. Mix until you have a smooth paste. This may take a couple of minutes depending on the power of your processor.

Once smooth, scoop the caramel into a sealable jar.

Using a knife/butter knife, cover the apples with the caramel sauce and pour 1 tbsp desiccated coconut for every apple. You can either pop the apples in the fridge for an hour to slightly harden up or dig in straight away (although, mind the stickiness!)

Health benefits of dates

Although I don't usually eat dates as part of my Primal diet, they are still a natural food source and therefore, we're not going against any Primal rules by consuming them. In fact, since dates were discovered thousands of years ago, they've been known to having healing powers. They're an amazing source of various vitamins and minerals, energy and fibre. And they also contain iron, calcium, phosphorus, magnesium, zinc and potassium. As for their health benefits, they contain quite a few...

- They can help lower cholesterol
- A source of protein
- Rich in vitamins including B1, B2, B3 and B5, as well as A1 and C
- Natural energy booster
- Can improve bone health
- Strengthens our nervous system thanks to their potassium content
- Promotes good digestion (especially soaked in water become consumption)

One thing I will say however is to bear in mind your portion control. Yes, dates may be good for us, but a little bit too much of anything is not healthy for us!

SUGAR-FREE DOUBLE CHOCOLATE CHIP MUFFINS

Number of servings: 12 muffins   Preparation Time: 10 minutes   Cooking Time: 25 minutes

We thought we'd prove to you that you can still have your Primal cake and eat it. How? By turning your favourite cakes into sugar-free recipes!

In fact, turning your favourite recipes into something a lot healthier really isn't as hard (nor tasteless) as many of you may think. It's all about making mindful swaps that are Primal-friendly. To give you the low down, here are a few Primal swaps that some of you should know about.

Ingredients

286g organic butternut squash (cooked and very soft)
1 vanilla pod
1 tbsp full fat milk or nut milk
2 eggs
60g *Primal Cure* coconut oil
200g almond flour

2 tbsp coconut flour
30g organic cacao powder
1 tsp baking soda
Pinch salt
150g 85% organic dark chocolate (chopped into square chunks)
95g raw honey

Method

Begin by preheating your oven to gas mark 4 (180 degrees Celsius) and pop 12 muffin cups in a muffin tray/onto a tray. In a food processor, add the butternut squash and honey and blitz together until you have a purée-like texture. Add the rest of the wet ingredients and mix.

In a separate bowl, add together the dry ingredients (excluding the chocolate chunks) and mix together.

Slowly, add the dry ingredients to the wet ingredients and mix until just combined. Add the dark chocolate chunks and mix again.

Pour the mixture evenly into each cup until all 12 cups are filled. Top with extra chocolate chunks if desired and then pop in the middle of the oven to bake for 25 minutes.

Once done, remove from the oven and leave to cool.

These muffins are best kept in an airtight container for a few days.

Primal tip

If you're making something that calls for caramel sauce then puréed organic dates make a delicious alternative. In fact, we much prefer this caramel date sauce than your sugary filled one! All you need to do in blend together a cups worth of pitted dates with a little water (or milk) and add a teaspoon of your favourite nut butter. Trust us, it's delicious!

PRIMAL HEALTH INDEX

Hippocrates famously said, "Let food be thy medicine, and medicine be thy food. Please use this health index to discover ingredients to include in your recipes that are believed to help prevent certain illnesses and indeed cure others; true *Primal Cure*. The index is not to replace advice from your doctor, nor prescribed medicines. It is also not exhaustive, but more of a snapshot. For example, we have mentioned 16 ingredients and foods that may contribute towards the prevention of cancer, yet there are dozens more mentioned in a multitude of research papers.

ACNE & SKIN
Basil 51, 98, 102, 124,182
Blueberries 37, 76, 78, 94
Carrots 38, 138, 144, 147, 156, 159, 187, 189, 192, 218
Coconut 48, 64, 68, 76, 86, 94, 98, 102, 109, 150, 176, 180, 198, 206, 216
Garlic 40, 66, 68, 98, 102, 106, 118, 134, 147, 15
Spinach 45, 66, 68, 74, 80, 82, 107, 118, 136, 140, 150
Turmeric 51, 87, 90, 98, 111, 114, 153

ARTHRITIS
Black Pepper 51
Blueberries 37, 76, 78, 94
Coconut 48, 64, 68, 76, 86, 94, 98, 102, 109, 150, 176, 180, 198, 206, 216
Fibre 32, 88, 168
Ginger 40, 72, 90, 93, 98, 214, 218
Omega 3 33, 138, 170
Oregano 51, 100, 124, 162, 182, 185
Pineapple 44, 98, 102, 159
Sesame Seeds 45
Spinach 5, 66, 68, 74, 80, 82, 107, 118, 136, 140, 150
Turmeric 51, 87, 90, 98, 111, 114, 153
Vanilla 51, 72, 78, 172, 200, 202, 208
Walnuts 46, 72, 170, 212, 218

ASTHMA
Broccoli 37, 98, 134, 140
Carrots 38, 138, 144, 147, 156, 159, 187, 189, 192, 218
Fibre 32, 88, 168
Garlic 40, 66, 68, 98, 102, 106, 118, 134, 147, 158
Magnesium 36, 44, 86, 173, 178
Mustard Seeds 51, 98
Omega 3 33, 138, 170
Pineapple 44, 98, 102, 159
Sesame Seeds 45
Sprouts 37, 128, 134
Tomatoes 66, 80, 107, 118, 122, 136, 142, 158, 162, 185

BLOOD SUGAR LEVELS
Cumin Seeds 51, 104, 106, 112, 142, 146, 154, 168
Flaxseeds 31, 40, 64, 104, 162, 172, 182
Garlic 40, 66, 68, 98, 102, 106, 118, 134, 147, 158
Mango 43, 150, 159
Onions 43, 82, 98, 102, 107, 110, 124, 132, 142, 154
Spring Onions 45, 109, 130, 132

BONES
Almonds 36, 64, 72, 76, 78, 87
Broccoli 37, 98, 134, 140
Cauliflower 38, 98, 104, 114, 132, 147, 150, 156, 190
Coconut 48, 64, 68, 76, 86, 94, 98, 102, 109, 150, 176, 180, 198, 206, 216
Eggs 40, 66, 74, 80, 82, 104, 114, 161
Pecan Nuts 43, 72, 176, 178
Salmon 44, 68, 74, 98, 126, 134, 140
Spring Onions 45, 109, 130, 132
Watercress 46, 66

CANCER
Basil 51, 98, 102, 124,182
Bell Peppers 37, 123, 132, 189
Blueberries 37, 76, 78, 94
Broccoli 37, 98, 134, 140
Cashews 38, 42, 170, 216,
Cauliflower 38, 98, 104, 114, 132, 147, 150, 156, 190
Cranberries 40, 128
Flaxseeds 31, 40, 64, 104, 162, 172, 182
Garlic 40, 66, 68, 98, 102, 106, 118, 134, 147, 158
Onions 43, 82, 98, 102, 107, 110, 124, 132, 142, 154
Paprika 51, 102, 106, 122, 146, 162, 186
Parsley 51, 80, 107, 122, 142, 158
Peanuts 43, 144, 159
Raspberries 44, 200
Tomatoes 66, 80, 107, 118, 122, 136, 142, 158, 162, 185
Turmeric 51, 87, 90, 98, 111, 114, 153

CHOLESTEROL (REDUCE LDL)
Apple Cider Vinegar 36, 107, 130, 182
Beef 37, 88, 102, 124, 142, 154, 156
Chicken 44, 110, 118, 122, 132, 136, 144, 150, 153, 159, 166
Flaxseeds 31, 40, 64, 104, 162, 172, 182
Sunflower Seeds 45, 172
Tuna 46

COGNITIVE (BRAIN)
Chia Seeds 38, 64, 70, 206, 216
Cod 38, 88, 109, 134, 155,
Coffee 40, 86, 178
Cranberries 40, 128
Eggs 102, 109, 150, 176, 180, 198, 206
Garlic 40, 66, 68, 98, 102, 106, 118, 134, 147, 158
Maca 51, 66, 76, 196, 220
Mango 43, 150, 159
Onions 43, 82, 98, 102, 107, 110, 124, 132, 142, 154
Raspberries 44, 200
Rosemary 51, 124, 138, 156, 190
Sardines 45
Shell Fish 45, 134, 149, 158

COLDS & FLU
Bell Peppers 37, 123, 132, 189
Garlic 40, 66, 68, 98, 102, 106, 118, 134, 147, 158
Mustard Seeds 51, 98
Thyme 51, 100, 138, 147, 166, 192
Turnips 46
Vitamin C 35
Zinc 35, 138, 221

DEPRESSION & ANXIETY
Goji Berries 40, 83, 89
Maca 51, 66, 76, 196, 220
Nutmeg 51, 166, 212, 214
Raspberries 44, 200
Sardines 45
Thyme 51, 100, 138, 147, 166, 192
Trout 46
Turmeric 51, 87, 90, 98, 111, 114, 153

For additional recipes and all of the latest advice and tips on living Primally, visit...

WWW.PRIMALCURE.COM

The website also offers a unique range of fine quality Primal ingredients, helping you achieve the very most out of your nutritious cooking.

With your very first order, no matter how small; even if it's just for a single jar of cocoa powder or flaxseed oil, we will send you a free copy of Steve's *book The Primal Cure* (*worth £9.99*), just use the code <u>GOURMET</u> at checkout.